Additional Praise for
The Hard Times Guide to Retirement Security
Practical Strategies for Money, Work, and Living

"Mark Miller is an all-around expert on encores, second-acts, and retirement in its many forms, as well as a gifted and eloquent writer. His new guide is as smart and resourceful as he is. Buy it, read it, and follow its wisdom to a better life!"

> —MARC FREEDMAN
> Author of *Encore: Finding Work That Matters in the Second Half of Life*

"The Hard Times Guide to Retirement is as important for the boomers to read today as Fun with Dick and Jane in 1955. It is the primer for the next phase of their life. No one understands the financial implications of the future of the boomers more than Mark Miller."

> —MARY FURLONG
> Author of *Turning Silver into Gold*

"This is the retirement book you need now. Rather than vague, empty promises, it gives you the stark truth. And then explains in concise, well-written prose, what to do about it. Miller is a sure-footed guide whose advice rings with authority."

> —MARY ROWLAND
> Author of *The New Commonsense Guide to Your 401(k)*

The Hard Times Guide to Retirement Security

The Hard Times Guide to Retirement Security

PRACTICAL STRATEGIES FOR MONEY, WORK, AND LIVING

MARK MILLER

BLOOMBERG PRESS
An Imprint of
WILEY

Published by John Wiley & Sons, Inc., Hoboken, New Jersey.
Published simultaneously in Canada.

For general information on our other products and services or for technical support, please contact our Customer Care Department within the United States at (800) 762-2974, outside the United States at (317) 572-3993 or fax (317) 572-4002.

Wiley also publishes its books in a variety of electronic formats. Some content that appears in print may not be available in electronic books. For more information about Wiley products, visit our web site at www.wiley.com.

ISBN 978-1-576-60362-8

Printed in the United States of America.

10 9 8 7 6 5 4 3 2 1

In memory of my parents, Marvin and Rayna Miller, dedicated activists for social justice. And with much love for Shira, Beth, and Asher, who will someday grow old, too. May they benefit from our generation's lessons learned.

Contents

Acknowledgments

I ENVISIONED *The Hard Times Guide to Retirement Security* as a survey of the best thinking on a wide array of subjects—everything from Social Security and pensions to health care, fifty-plus careers, entrepreneurship, and volunteering. As such, I relied on experts in many different fields for guidance. Many were generous with their time, sharing information and research and agreeing to review and comment on chapters. My sincere thanks go to Andrew Eschtruth, associate director for external relations at the Center for Retirement Research at Boston College; Christine Fahlund and Stuart Ritter, financial planners at T. Rowe Price; Sheryl Garrett, founder of the Garrett Planning Network; Alan Glickstein, senior consultant at Watson Wyatt; Martha Holstein, ethicist at the Health and Medicine Policy Research Group; Cindy Hounsell, director of the Women's Institute for a Secure Retirement; Marika and Howard Stone, principals of 2Young2Retire; Steve Vernon, president of Rest-of-Life Communications; and Jeff Williams, principal at Bizstarters.com.

Others who provided invaluable assistance by reviewing and commenting on early drafts of the book include Dan Cornfield, Jane Kaplan, Bob Handler, Susan and Steve Varick, and Lila Weinberg.

I'd also like to thank two other writers who coached me through this first experience with book publishing—my friends Steve Fiffer and Jane Kaplan. The advice of my agent, Lynn Haller at Studio B, also was invaluable. I'm also indebted to Stephen Isaacs, my editor at Bloomberg Press, for his guidance.

As always, my best and first editor was my wonderful and wise wife—and best friend—Anita Weinberg.

The Hard Times Guide to Retirement Security

CHAPTER 1

Rethinking Retirement in Hard Times

THE TIMING COULDN'T BE WORSE: The largest generation in our history is approaching retirement age during the worst economic downturn since the Great Depression.

Before the economy crashed, many baby boomers had been holding on to vague notions that retirement would somehow work itself out through their good luck in real estate, in the stock market, or by inheritance.

Whatever the reason, most Americans before they retire have paid little attention to the huge life transition that is coming. We don't have a good idea of how much we need to save for retirement; only 44 percent of workers responding to one survey said they had tried to calculate what they would need, and an equal number simply "guess at how much they will need" for a comfortable retirement.[1] Another survey of Americans 56 to 65 years old showed that almost half of the respondents underestimated the amount of retirement income they would need, and nearly 70 percent overestimated how much they could draw down from their retirement savings annually.[2] Sixty percent underestimated their odds of living beyond a given average life expectancy. Meanwhile, about half of Americans file for Social Security benefits too early, often cheating themselves out of hundreds of thousands of dollars in lifetime benefits. Only half of all working adults participate in a workplace retirement-savings program. And the average U.S. household has managed to save just $60,000 toward retirement.[3]

Now the crash has ushered in a new economic reality that will be with us for years to come. Real estate values and retirement portfolios are depressed, and job security has evaporated. And even though the economy surely will recover, we're not likely to see the type of sharp bounce-back that characterized the end of many previous recessions. That means anyone planning to leave the workforce in the next five to ten years will be retiring into an economy that looks much as it does today.

The need to build retirement security has never been greater. But one of the main obstacles is the current *concept* of retirement—the idea that people should stop working in their early sixties and take it easy. The number of years that you'll have to fund after you stop working is one of the most important variables affecting retirement security. Paying for retirement has become more challenging in light of recession-ravaged 401(k)s and plunging housing values. And those resources must be spread over a rising number of years. American life expectancy has been expanding at an astonishing rate. An American man turning age 65 in 1940—just a few years after Social Security was enacted—could expect to live an average of another 11.9 years; by 2006, that number had jumped to 16.5 years. For women, the corresponding life expectancy had jumped from 13.4 years to 19.1 years.[4] Those are just average figures, which means that half of us will live much longer. And the Social Security Administration projects that average life expectancy will keep rising in the decades ahead.

That's good news, of course—but how will we pay for all those additional years of retirement?

The idea of quitting work at a predetermined age dates back to nineteenth-century Germany, where the first system of social security was created in 1889. The system was funded by mandatory contributions from employers and employees, and citizens would be eligible to receive benefits at age 70, an age that was later reduced to 65.[5] The German system later served as a role model for the U.S. Social Security system that President Franklin D. Roosevelt created during the Great Depression. FDR envisioned Social Security as a response to that era's widespread poverty, signing it into law in 1935 as part of broader legislation that provided for unemployment insurance, old-age assistance, and aid to dependent children. Like the German system, our Social Security law pegged 65 as the age when Americans could retire and begin receiving benefits. That set the stage for widespread expansion of private pensions after World War II, especially in unionized industries such as the Detroit carmakers. By the 1950s, the idea that people should be able to quit work and adopt a leisure-centered lifestyle after age 65 had gained widespread acceptance—and it's been with us ever since.

That approach no longer seems sustainable. The economic downturn, coupled with increased life expectancy, points toward longer working lives for older Americans. That won't be easy to achieve in a weak economy with high unemployment rates, but staying on the job even a few years beyond traditional retirement age can make a tremendous difference in achieving long-term retirement security.

There are no magic bullets or easy solutions to the problem of retirement security. Yet in my work as a journalist covering retirement and aging, I'm often struck by the wealth of good ideas that experts have identified for achieving a satisfying, secure retirement—even in hard times. These aren't get-rich-quick investment gimmicks, schemes to make millions working part-time from your kitchen table, or come-ons to retire cheaply in Central America. Rather, the best ideas focus on basic blocking and tackling—getting the most from the financial tools already at hand, and making smart decisions about work and lifestyle.

This book explores ways to achieve long-term retirement security, which I define as reliably generating income to support a retirement that could well last 25 years or more for you or your spouse. The generation of Americans now approaching retirement needs to begin focusing on what lies ahead. Boomers need to get smarter—quickly—about retirement.

Money

Over the past several decades, retirement *finance* has become synonymous with retirement *investing*. But it's worth remembering that individually controlled retirement-investment accounts haven't always been with us. The 401(k) and individual retirement account only arrived on the scene in the 1980s. At the time, about 38 percent of private-sector American workers still participated in traditional, defined benefit pensions that were funded and managed by employers and that provided regular lifetime checks after retirement. Over the years, the balance shifted dramatically toward defined contribution plans—mainly 401(k)s—in which employers commit to a specific contribution of funds but leave employees free to manage the invested funds and make their own contributions. By 2008, only 20 percent of workers had a defined benefit pension,[6] although a larger percentage of large companies still offered them.

Defined contribution (DC) plans have never come close to replacing defined benefit pensions as a source of retirement security. Simply put, the DC pension system just isn't getting the job done, for the following reasons.

➤ Only 56 percent of American workers are active participants in a DC plan. One major reason is access; no law mandates that employers offer 401(k)s, and about 35 percent of workers don't have access to an employer-sponsored plan. Choice is another factor; 15 percent of workers who have access to a 401(k) decline to participate. More than 70 percent of low-income households reach retirement age without any employer-sponsored retirement coverage.[7]

➤ Employers are cutting back on matching contributions. In 2008, one-third of employers reduced or eliminated their matching contributions to retirement accounts, and another 29 percent planned to do so in 2009.[8]

➤ On average, employees contribute 7.5 percent of their salaries,[9] about half the rate recommended by most financial planning experts.

➤ Exposure to stocks is too great as retirement approaches. Nearly one in four investors approaching retirement age (56–65) had more than 90 percent of their account balances in equities at the end of 2007.[10] That's far too high, and older investors suffered huge losses when the market crashed in 2008.

➤ Investors cash out prematurely. About 45 percent of plan participants cash out their 401(k) balances when they change jobs rather than roll them over to new employers or IRAs.[11] That disrupts the long-term growth of their assets. Borrowing and hardship withdrawals also are allowed under the rules, and people have been tapping into their balances somewhat more frequently during the economic crisis.

All these factors add up to woeful underperformance by the defined contribution system. In 2007—before the crash—the median amount saved by households headed by a person in the preretirement years (54–65) was $50,500—just 7 percent of total household wealth.[12]

It's time to hit the reset button and pay attention to the broader array of financial tools that can help build retirement security.

Social Security

For most of us, Social Security will be the bedrock of retirement income. The program won't disappear into insolvency anytime soon, despite the politically motivated forecasts of doom we hear from time to time. But Americans do need to get smarter about maximizing their benefits. Most don't know when they become eligible for Social Security, how much it pays, or when it makes the most sense to file for benefits. Good planning and decision making can add hundreds of thousands of dollars to lifetime benefits for you and your spouse.

Pensions

Although they've been waning, defined benefit pensions remain a very big part of the American retirement-security system. Pension plans have generated a good deal of bad press in recent years because of a series of catastrophic, high-profile failures of big plans at companies such as United Airlines and Bethlehem Steel. But if you do have a defined benefit pension, it's going to be a key underpinning of your retirement-security plan; and the best part is that it mostly flies on automatic pilot. Still, it's important to gauge the safety and stability of your employer's plan and the variety of benefits for which you may qualify.

Income Annuities

Americans without traditional pensions face the challenge of meeting retirement expenses with a combination of Social Security and savings. But one overlooked option is purchasing a do-it-yourself pension—otherwise known as an *income annuity*. Simply put, you make a single payment up front to an insurance company and begin receiving payments immediately; the price depends on factors such as your age at the time of purchase, gender, survivor benefits, and whether you want the payments to last for a fixed period of time or the rest of your life. Income annuities haven't gained widespread popularity as financial tools for retirement, mainly because people dislike losing control of their assets and worry that they won't "make back" the large sum of money that must be invested up front. However, used properly, an income annuity is an effective tool for covering basic living expenses and can provide effective insurance against the risk of outliving your money.

Recalibrating Portfolios

Are you one of those people who have been stuffing unopened 401(k) statements into a file drawer? Well done! While denial isn't much of an investment strategy, the key to coping with the market crash is taking a long-term view. The goal is to make sure your retirement nest egg lasts many years into the future. If you're younger than 50, you've got time for the market to bounce back; the key here is to keep saving and to keep your portfolio balanced through use of tools such as target date funds, which automatically shift to a more conservative investment mix as retirement approaches. For older investors close to retirement—or already retired—the challenge is more difficult because it involves some belt tightening. The most effective strategies call for delaying your retirement and adjusting your rate of annual withdrawals.

Health Care

If you're over age 65, Medicare provides an important health-care safety net. But the economic crisis has forcibly retired millions of Americans in their fifties and sixties, leaving them without health insurance. Even for those on Medicare, health-care costs are eroding spending power and economic security; out-of-pocket expenses for people in retirement have jumped 50 percent since 2002.[13] Health-care expense poses one of the most important risks to retirement security, so it's important to understand how to navigate the system and mitigate expense risk.

Taxes

Yes, you'll still owe taxes in retirement. Your income may well be lower, which will lighten your income tax burden, but several new factors come into play that affect your tax situation; these concern retirement savings, Social Security, and any continued income from continuing to work. You'll need to make a number of key tax-related decisions starting the day you retire.

Real Estate

Older Americans have a higher rate of home ownership than any other demographic group, and we're just beginning to come to terms with a housing market that has changed for the foreseeable future. In some parts of the country, prices are down more than 30 percent from their peak,[14] and the impact on boomers has been dramatic. One recent study suggested that 30 percent of Americans ages 45 to 54 are "underwater" on their mortgages—that is, they owe more than their homes are worth and would need to bring cash to a closing.[15] With today's high unemployment rates, sagging incomes, and rising foreclosure rates, we're not likely to see a strong rebound in housing anytime soon—and that's a challenge for anyone who needs to sell for retirement-related reasons. But planning for your housing needs in retirement brings into play a number of lifestyle considerations that have little to do with the current market. Is a move right for you, or can your current residence be adapted to serve your needs? What role can technology play in your retirement dwelling? Can you cut your expenses—dramatically—by paying off the mortgage before you retire?

Advice

Even before the economic crash, the boomer retirement knowledge gap was large, and the need for smart planning has only become more acute in hard times. Do-it-yourself planning certainly is an option, but a little help from a professional adviser can be well worth the time and money. The rationale for hiring a trustworthy adviser is simple: Money spent now could make a big difference in helping you achieve a secure, happy future retirement. But finding a savvy adviser is a big challenge; almost anyone can hang out a shingle and start handing out advice. Planners may have any number of certifications or titles attached to their names, but none are required. So you'll need to understand the various types of advisory services that are available and how to interview and hire an adviser.

Work

Working in retirement: It sounds like a contradiction in terms. But most boomers weren't envisioning a retreat from work at retirement age even before the economy crashed. Boomers have been telling just about anyone who would listen that they want to reinvent their careers and forge a new style of aging centered around an active, engaged, and productive lifestyle. Those aspirations are consistent with the boomer generation's history of rebellious behavior (in their youth, at least). But rising longevity and the chance to live a greater number of healthy, productive years are additional factors making the "bonus round"[16] an opportunity that is too enticing to pass up.

Here's the problem: Most boomers don't have a clue how to pull off this type of profound life transition. The personal upheaval associated with career transition can't be overstated, especially for those grappling with an unexpected, premature job loss. Sorting out the choices can be daunting, and many of us don't know how to get started. Many also feel additional pressure to "get it right" because this may well be the last career switch.

Work Longer, Not Forever

Working even a few years beyond what you've planned can pay a surprisingly large bonus in retirement security. Age 66 is the normal retirement age (NRA) for most people, as defined by Social Security, but about half of all Americans don't wait that long. You can avoid the early-filing benefit reductions imposed by Social Security by working until your NRA. At the same time, you can keep contributing to your retirement-savings plan, building additional balances that can be put to work in the market. And every additional year of working income is a year in which you're not supporting yourself by drawing down retirement balances. *The upshot is that staying on the job a few additional years can boost your income in retirement by one-third or more.*

Corporate America after Age 50

If you think you'll want to stay in the mainstream business world, working as a Wal-Mart greeter isn't your only option. But the employment outlook for older workers is mixed at best. Employers say they value older workers' experience, knowledge, and loyalty; and it's clear they are prized in some fields of work. But it's just as clear that employment security is eroding for older workers and that age discrimination is a major hurdle to staying employed. Success in the workplace depends on getting a realistic handle on corporate attitudes toward older workers and understanding where the best opportunities lie.

Job Hunting

Keeping or finding a job is challenging for anyone in tough economic times, but it's harder if you're over age 50—a reality that is colliding with older workers' intention to stick around. Experts in human resources—as well as successful older job seekers—assert that it can be done. But in this economy, older workers will need to adopt new strategies for staying employed and selling themselves after age 50.

Starting a Business

Many boomers who want to keep working will wind up launching their own businesses. In some cases, that will mean launching full-blown companies requiring significant start-up capital, office space, employees, and all the accompanying headaches. Others will start "lifestyle businesses"—small ventures that can be launched with minimum capital and that balance work, play, and other pursuits. Lifestyle businesses can be started without much start-up capital—a big plus in a difficult economy. Still, these businesses may not generate much revenue immediately. That means lifestyle entrepreneurs need to maintain an adequate cash cushion to fund their living expenses while starting up.

Living

Hard times require belt-tightening, but the new retirement won't all be about money and work. With the country facing economic, environmental, educational, and other simultaneous crises, boomers are weighing the legacy that they will leave to the next generation and looking for ways to give back—a trend that is playing out in their careers and in the way they spend free time.

Encore Careers

Before the economy crashed, millions of midlife adults already were starting new careers in fields where they hoped to make a positive social contribution in areas such as teaching, health care, government, and the not-for-profit world. The tough economy hasn't really forced people to give up on the dream of second careers with meaning; if anything, their resolve seems to be growing. These "encore careers" can be found anywhere there's a clear social need that fits your passions and interests. But some fields have surfaced as clear early adopters of the encore career concept. Best of all, they're fields that are growing and hiring.

Volunteering and Public Service

The number of older Americans volunteering their time has never been higher. The impulse toward public service and civic engagement is partly a response to the terrorist attacks on September 11, 2001, and natural disasters such as Hurricane Katrina and the 2004 tsunami.[17] The recession also is a factor; out-of-work Americans have been volunteering at record levels as a way to keep busy and engaged while they hunt for paid positions. They're learning that volunteering offers a chance to learn new skills, feel valued, and leverage the skills learned in previous jobs. There are other benefits, as well; one study of volunteers found that volunteers had better mental and physical health, were more physically active, and had higher self-esteem as a result of their participation.[18] The trend encompasses work being done here at home and abroad. A wide range of not-for-profit, charitable organizations and businesses has sprung up that cater to the "voluntourism" market. Some older Americans have even made the commitment to join the Peace Corps.

Lifelong Learning

Heading back to the classroom has long been popular as an enrichment activity in retirement. Adult learning can transform lives and lead to new careers, but it's also becoming clear that there's a link between learning, health, and general well-being that stems from keeping the brain challenged. The options include self-directed programs at Lifelong Learning Institutes as well as traditional continuing education and educational travel.

———•·•———

The aim of this book is to offer a realistic assessment of how the emerging economy will affect the generation of Americans now approaching retirement, as well as help readers boost their retirement IQs by showcasing the best thinking I've been able to find in my reporting on retirement and aging. The result, I hope you'll agree, is a comprehensive guide to strategies for building retirement security in hard times.

Chapter Notes

1. Ruth Helman, Craig Copeland, and Jack VanDerhei, "The 2009 Retirement Confidence Survey: Economy Drives Confidence to Record Lows; Many Looking to Work Longer," *EBRI Issue Brief*, no. 328 (April 2009) (www.ebri.org/publications/ib/index.cfm?fa=ibDisp&content_id=4226), accessed September 2009.

2. MetLife Mature Market Institute Retirement Income IQ Test.

3. Alicia H. Munnell, Francesca Golub-Sass, and Dan Muldoon, *An Update on 401(k) Plans: Insights from the 2007 SCF* (Chestnut Hill, MA: Center for Retirement Research at Boston College, March 2009).

4. Social Security Administration, 2007 OASDI Trustees Report (www.ssa.gov/OACT/TR/TR07/V_demographic.html), accessed September 2009.

5. Kenneth Silber, "From Bismarck to Bush," *Research Magazine*, July 31, 2008.

6. Barbara A. Butrica, Howard M. Iams, Karen E. Smith, and Eric J. Toder, *The Disappearing Defined Benefit Pension and Its Potential Impact on the Retirement Incomes of Boomers* (Washington, DC: The Urban Institute, January 2009), p. 5 (www.ssa.gov/policy/docs/ssb/v69n3/v69n3p1.html).

7. Robert Stowe England, "Principles for a New Retirement System," *Retirement USA* (March 10, 2009), p. 5 (www.cpcpac.com/090310-working-paper-finalpdf1%5B1%5D.pdf) accessed June 2009.

8. Spectrem Group, "One-Third of U.S. Employers Have Reduced or Eliminated Retirement Plan Matches in Economic Crisis" (March 25, 2009) (www.spectrem.com/custom.aspx?id=96), accessed September 2009.

9. Employee Benefits Research Institute, "Average Worker Contribution Rates to 401(k)-Type Plans" (March 2009) (www.ebri.org/pdf/FFE117.19March09.Final.pdf), accessed June 2009.

10. Jack VanDerhei, "The Impact of the Recent Financial Crisis on 401(k) Account Balances," *EBRI Issue Brief*, no. 326 (February 2009)

(www.ebri.org/publications/ib/index.cfm?fa=ibDisp&content _id=4192), accessed June 2009.

11. Alicia H. Munnell, Francesca Golub-Sass, and Dan Muldoon, *An Update on 401(k) Plans: Insights from the 2007 SCF* (Chestnut Hill, MA: Center for Retirement Research at Boston College, March 2009).

12. Munnell, Golub-Sass, and Muldoon.

13. Fidelity Investments, "Paying for Health Care in Retirement" (April 24, 2009) (http://publications.fidelity.com/investorsWeekly/application/ loadArticle?pagename=IW090417health), accessed September 2009.

14. John F. Wasik, "U.S. Home Prices May Be Lost for a Generation," *Bloomberg News* (May 4, 2009) (www.bloomberg.com/apps/ news?pid=20601039&sid=aiiT.sNeq2YQ), accessed July 2009.

15. David Rosnick and Dean Baker, *The Wealth of the Baby Boom Cohorts After the Collapse of the Housing Bubble* (Washington, DC: Center for Economic and Policy Research, February 2009) (www .cepr.net/index.php/publications/reports/the-wealth-of-the-baby -boom-cohorts-after-the-collapse-of-the-housing-bubble/), accessed July 2009.

16. Mary Furlong, *Turning Silver into Gold: How to Profit in the New Boomer Marketplace* (New York: FT Press, 2009), p. 9.

17. Robert Grimm Jr., Nathan Dietz, John Foster-Bey, David Reingold, and Rebecca Nesbit, *Volunteer Growth in America: A Review of Trends Since 1974* (Washington, DC: Corporation for National and Community Service, December 2006), p. 5.

18. Nancy Morrow-Howell, Song-Iee Hong, Stacey McCrary, and Wayne Blinne, *Experience Corps: Health Outcomes of Participation* (St. Louis: Washington University, George Warren Brown School of Social Work, February 2009) (www.experiencecorps.org/impact/ for_members.cfm), accessed August 2009.

Money

CHAPTER 2

The Great
Wake-Up Call

THE GREAT RECESSION HAS sent a wake-up call to older Americans.

We're adjusting our expectations, getting sober, and starting to focus on the nuts and bolts of planning for retirement. The dramatic erosion of wealth also has prompted us to focus more on lifestyle, experiences, and personal values. "People are not just looking at what they have, but at how they will live," says Laura Rossman, an expert on marketing to boomers and seniors. "They're realizing that they may need to put off retirement and getting realistic about what it takes. The market drop has been severe, and no one ever expected anything like the severity of the shock. It is changing some behaviors, and people are resetting their views."

Confidence about retirement security has plunged. The Employee Benefit Research Institute (EBRI) has been surveying Americans annually for 16 years on their attitudes about retirement. In 2009, the percentage of respondents who said they were confident that they would have enough money to retire comfortably stood at the lowest point since the first survey in 1993.[1] In general, EBRI's findings reflect a striking new sense of seriousness in attitudes about retirement.

➤ **Delaying retirement:** People plan to work longer to secure their retirement; 28 percent said they had changed their target year for retirement in the past year, with most (89 percent) saying they were doing so to boost their financial security.

➤ **Working in retirement:** More people plan to supplement their income in retirement by working—72 percent compared with 66 percent two years ago and before the economy crashed.

➤ **Getting serious about managing money:** Among those who've lost confidence in their future retirement security, 81 percent said they had cut spending, and 43 percent changed the way they invest. And 75 percent of those surveyed said they are saving money for retirement, one of the highest numbers EBRI has ever measured.

Rossman sees evidence of broader changes in the way people approach retirement. There's less focus on moving away to retirement communities—in part because of the depressed housing market, but also because of a heightened focus on intergenerational dependence.

"It wasn't that unusual in the 1940s or 1950s to see families living together across generations. It's hardly a new concept to have grandma in the house or kids sticking around longer. But now we're starting to see a new openness to sharing resources and not feeling that you need to prove you have it all."

Finally, Rossman sees a new attitude emerging about retirement. "It's going to be an era of simplicity and new priorities—less is more."

These new attitudes point toward a need for fresh thinking about the financial aspects of retirement security. The old approach, pushed often and hard by the financial services industry, is the income-replacement rule of thumb: To retire comfortably, you'll need to replace about 80 percent of annual income. At best, the income-replacement method is a crude estimate. It doesn't, for example, take into account unforeseen spending needs that could require higher sums, such as health care or long-term care expenses.

But most important, the income-replacement method is wrong for an economy in hard times because it doesn't start with the right questions: *What is the lifestyle I want? How much will I need to spend on basics? What can I afford to spend in this economy?*

"The replacement ratio method is a good place to start, but it ignores major changes that can result from reduced expenses for dependent children, paying off a mortgage, or downsizing major items like your home or cars," says Steve Vernon, an actuary and president of Rest-of-Life Communications, a retirement-education concern. "It also assumes you'll want the same material standard of living in retirement that you had before.

That ignores the possibility that you might be willing to live on less. Often, as people age, they're less interested in material things and more interested in learning, hobbies, volunteering, and spending time with friends and family."

A better approach in hard times is to start with a clean slate. Take the time to create a budget of foreseeable expenses, and balance those expenses against the sources of income that you can count on.

The first step is getting a precise handle on what you currently spend. You can do that by using any of the major financial-planning software tools or by tracking what you spend on a spreadsheet for a couple of months. Working with a trusted financial planner is another good way to understand your spending patterns.

Once you've got a good picture of current spending, subtract any regular expenses that won't continue in retirement—for instance, the cost of commuting, dry-cleaning bills, and taxes for Medicare and Social Security. Then, you'll need to take into account areas of spending likely to be higher in retirement. Health-care expenditures almost certainly will be higher (see Chapter 7), and if you hope to travel extensively or make other lifestyle changes, do your best to estimate those costs, too.

Housing decisions can be key in simplifying retirement income needs. Despite all the marketing hype about retirement living and stereotypes about Florida retirees, most Americans actually don't spend a great deal of money on retirement property but prefer to stay where they are, aging in place during retirement. Those who do move stay within a 20-mile distance of their previous home, which suggests that they're merely downsizing.[2] Paying off a mortgage before retiring can be another great way to reduce your recurring expenses in retirement, even if it means using cash on hand; the interest expense almost certainly will be greater than the returns you'd earn on low-risk fixed-income investments.

Resources

Choose to Save Ballpark Estimate. This simple online worksheet helps you calculate how much you need to save. The ballpark calculator focuses on boiling down complex issues such as projected Social Security benefits and earning assumptions on your savings. Choose to Save is a project of the Employee Benefit Research Institute (http://choosetosave .org/ballpark/).

Mint.com. This free personal finance Web site (www.mint.com/) allows you to download your bank and credit card data and analyze where your money goes.

Social Security Retirement Estimator. The Social Security Administration has built a useful online tool (at www.socialsecurity.gov/estimator/) that allows you to project your personal future benefits assuming different retirement ages.

Chapter Notes

1. Ruth Helman, Craig Copeland, and Jack VanDerhei, "The 2009 Retirement Confidence Survey: Economy Drives Confidence to Record Lows; Many Looking to Work Longer," *EBRI Issue Brief*, no. 328 (April 2009) (www.ebri.org/publications/ib/index .cfm?fa=ibDisp&content_id=4226), accessed September 2009.

2. Kelly Haverstick and Natalia A. Zhivan, *Older Americans On the Go: How Often, Where and Why?* (Chestnut Hill, MA: Center for Retirement Research, September 2009) (http://crr.bc.edu/briefs/ older_americans_on_the_go_how_often_where_and_why_.html), accessed September 2009.

CHAPTER 3

Getting the Most from Social Security

CONSIDERING ALL THE ATTENTION the financial press pays to the stock market and investing for retirement, you'd think it's the most important source of retirement security. It's not. For most people, stock portfolios provide a relatively small portion of overall income in retirement; the average American household approaches retirement with about $60,000 in retirement portfolio savings,[1] hardly enough to play a central role in retirement-security planning. And traditional pension plans are a disappearing breed. That means most Americans will rely on Social Security as their most important source of support in retirement—39 percent of total income on average.[2] It's a terribly important resource—and one that most of us don't understand very well. Most Americans don't know when they become eligible for Social Security, how much it pays, or how to maximize benefits.

Against the backdrop of the economic crash, it's hard to overstate the importance of Social Security as a key component of retirement security. You've been paying taxes into the system your entire working life, and payouts represent a sort of public annuity-style benefit that's there for you so long as you live. It's one of the few retirement benefits that automatically adjusts payments for inflation. And your benefits can be passed along to your spouse after you die. The program is absolutely critical for older Americans, keeping 35 percent of the elderly out of poverty.[3] It's the sole source of income for 42 percent of single women over age 62, and it accounts for as much as 80 percent of retirement income for people in low economic brackets.[4] Social Security also pays benefits to disabled Americans; about 17 percent of benefits paid out go to people who have been unable to work for at least a year because of a physical or mental impairment.[5]

For perspective, think of Social Security as a financial asset with actual value. What's it worth? The National Academy of Social Insurance (NASI) took a shot at answering this question.

According to the National Academy of Social Insurance, "The average Social Security benefit for a retiree is about $1,045 a month [in January 2007, NASI found]. If at age 65 you wanted to buy a contract from an insurance company to pay you $1,045 a month for the rest of your life, you would need $140,000 in cash. That would be the price of the contract, called a *fixed life annuity*. If you also wanted partial protection against inflation—a guarantee that the payments to you would rise 3 percent a year for the rest of your life—the price of the annuity would jump to $190,000. If, in addition, you wanted protection for your spouse—a guarantee that the payments would continue to your spouse after you die—the purchase price would rise to $225,000. This is a measure of the wealth value of Social Security for an average retiree today."[6]

Social Security was created by President Franklin D. Roosevelt in response to the widespread poverty of the Great Depression, and it was signed into law in 1935 as part of broader legislation that provided for unemployment insurance, old-age assistance, and aid to dependent children. Roosevelt viewed Social Security as a way to lift older Americans out of poverty, which afflicted about half of all seniors at the time. Although it marked the first significant introduction of European-style social insurance in the United States, Roosevelt's plan was far more moderate politically than an array of grassroots, populist plans proposed at the time. Some of these plans called for welfare-style, government-guaranteed pensions, but Social Security's funding would rely on a contributory system funded through payroll taxes.[7] The program isn't need based; it's an entitlement that we earn through those contributions.

Is Social Security in Trouble?

Social Security has been tremendously successful in reducing poverty among the elderly, but it has run into fiscal trouble from time to time, and we're at one of those moments now. The program is designed to be

Social Security Frequently Asked Questions

Qualifying for benefits. Benefits are calculated on a credit system that reflects the number of years an applicant has worked. Everyone who has worked for ten years and has a Social Security number is qualified for future payments. The benefits are based on your earnings and averaged over your working lifetime.

Applying for benefits. The Social Security Administration makes it possible to apply online, by telephone, or in person at a local office of the agency (see this chapter's Resources section).

When to apply. You can apply for benefits when you turn age 62, but keep in mind this could result in lower lifetime benefits, as described elsewhere in this chapter. Learn more at www.socialsecurity.gov/retire2/otherthings.htm.

Continue Work, Get Benefits

Can you work and receive Social Security benefits at the same time? It depends on your age.

If you've reached your normal retirement age (NRA), you can work and earn as much as you like and still receive full benefits. If you are younger than your NRA and if your earnings exceed a certain amount, some of your benefits will be withheld; $1 will be deducted from your benefit payments for every $2 you earn above the annual limit, which was $14,160 in 2009. But even then, your lifetime benefits wouldn't be reduced because the withheld benefits would be added to your benefits after you reach NRA.

The Social Security Administration offers an online calculator (at www.ssa.gov/OACT/COLA/RTeffect.html) that can help you figure your benefit reductions if you decide to work and collect benefits below your NRA.

self-financing and uses the Social Security Trust Fund to manage incoming payments and outgoing benefit payments. The main funding source is the federal payroll tax, which is set at 6.2 percent for both workers and employers—a combined 12.4 percent rate. Some upper-income Social Security beneficiaries also pay income taxes on their benefits to the fund.[8]

Projections show that taxes soon will no longer produce enough income to cover future benefit payments and that the trust fund will be depleted in 2037. The problem is the looming retirement of the huge baby-boomer generation, which is already starting to retire and draw benefits.

Social Security's potential, *theoretical* insolvency has generated a great deal of unhelpful political heat; it's often characterized as an immediate crisis and used as a basis for campaign scare tactics targeting seniors worried about their benefits. The Bush administration pointed to the program's fiscal problems in 2001 when it proposed partial privatization of Social Security—a plan that would have allowed people to put some of their Social Security dollars into private savings accounts, where the funds could be invested in mutual funds or other investments. That idea flopped with Republicans and Democrats alike. It's also a generational wedge issue, with some politicians portraying the program as an entitlement albatross hanging from the collective necks of young people who will never collect benefits themselves.

But policy makers have a number of clear options for getting Social Security back on solid long-term footing. In fact, most federal budget experts view Social Security as a manageable problem compared with the other big entitlement program, Medicare, which faces the same challenges bedeviling our broader health-care system. A Social Security fix won't be politically easy; it will involve increased taxes, trimmed benefits, or—most likely—some combination of the two. The benefit reduction ideas that have been floated include raising the normal retirement age (NRA), when full benefits can be received, and changing the formulas currently used for determining purchasing power or cost-of-living adjustments. On the revenue side, the possibilities include higher payroll taxes or reducing the cap on individuals whose benefits are subject to income tax (set at $106,800 for 2009).[9]

President Barack Obama has promised that Social Security reform will be a priority for his administration. As a candidate, Obama made clear that he opposed the privatization options pushed by Republicans.

Although Obama hasn't articulated specific plans, the administration seems to be leaning toward an increase in payroll taxes and some benefits reduction to restore the program's fiscal health.

Maximizing Your Benefits

No matter what changes are made, it's a sure bet Social Security isn't going away anytime soon—and it's 100 percent certain that the program will be one of your most important sources of security in retirement. But the amount you'll receive over the course of your retirement isn't assured or automatic. Maximizing your Social Security benefits will require some good planning and decision making.

The most important decision you'll make is when to enroll. Dozens of news stories appeared in January 2007 when the country's oldest baby boomer turned 62 and promptly signed up for Social Security. But it probably wasn't a very smart financial move. About half of all Americans do file at 62—the first year of eligibility for benefits. But for most people, it's a costly mistake that will mean forgoing thousands of dollars in lifetime benefits—in some cases, hundreds of thousands. Although you can file for benefits at 62, most Americans will receive larger lifetime payouts by waiting, if at all possible, until they reach age 66—or even 70. But it's a bit of a gamble, because the math all depends on how long you live.

Remember that Social Security is a public insurance program. It's built around actuarial principles—essentially, the mathematics of risk. And a central actuarial idea behind Social Security is the NRA, a rule used by the Social Security Administration (SSA) not only to ensure the system pays out fairly among all beneficiaries but also to ensure that funding is adequate as the longevity of the average American increases. The NRA has been rising gradually over the years; currently, it is age 66 for anyone born from 1943 to 1954, and slightly older for people born thereafter.

If you file for benefits early—that is, before the typical NRA of 66—the government reduces your benefit accordingly to avoid paying higher life-time benefits to you than it does to someone who waits until their NRA. Under the rules, your lifetime benefits will be reduced based on an actuarial projection of your longevity. Let's say your NRA is 66 but you retired and started taking Social Security at 62. That means you retired four years early. The net effect: Your annual benefits will be reduced permanently by a total of 25 percent.

On the other hand, SSA's rules offer incentives for you to wait past your NRA. The SSA will bump up your payment an additional amount for every year you delay filing for benefits. The net effect is that if you wait until age 70, your annual benefit will be 32 percent higher than it would be if you started at age 66—and you also get all the cost-of-living adjustments (COLAs) from the intervening years. You'll come out ahead so long as you—or your spouse—live past what's called the *break-even age*. That's the age where the total benefits paid to those who are patient begin to exceed total payouts to those who take early benefits. That age is around 80—and in the case of more than 80 percent of American couples, the husband or wife will live past that age.

The Case of the Vanishing Social Security COLA

One of Social Security's best features is inflation protection. By law, Social Security passes along an annual cost-of-living adjustment—or COLA—to recipients. Each annual increase is tied to a broad measure of inflation in the economy.

But the Great Recession is putting the squeeze on the Social Security COLA. Consumer prices have flattened out due to the sinking economy. Government forecasts make clear that Social Security recipients won't receive a COLA again before 2012 at the earliest. The situation might look like a wash at first glance; if consumer prices are flat, seniors don't need a raise, right? But retirees feel a disproportionate impact from a subset of prices that tend to rise more quickly than inflation in the broader economy: energy, transportation, and especially heath care. They're also grappling with the bad timing of falling home values and investment losses at a time when many need to tap those assets.

The result is that the vanishing COLA will squeeze many retirees hard—with health-care expenses exerting much of the pressure. This is due to the direct link between Social Security and Medicare premiums and other rising out-of-pocket costs.

Most Social Security recipients choose to have their Medicare Part B premiums deducted from their checks. Part B covers physician and nursing services, tests, vaccinations, and a variety of therapies; and the COLA normally is more than enough to cover any annual premium increases.

The Part B premium has been rising sharply in recent years. It was set at $96.40 per month in 2009 and jumped to $110.50 in 2010.

The good news is that about 75 percent of Medicare recipients are protected from a net decrease in benefits under a hold-harmless provision in federal law. But you're not protected from the increase if you fall into one of these categories:

➤ **High income**—individuals with modified adjusted gross incomes above $85,000, and couples above $170,000.
➤ **New enrollees**—new Social Security recipients who haven't seen an increase or decrease in benefits since they weren't getting payments in the previous year or weren't covered under Part B.
➤ **Medicaid recipients**—low-income individuals eligible for Medicaid and Medicare; in these situations, Medicaid pays the Part B premium.

Meanwhile, anyone participating in a Part D prescription drug program—which is voluntary—won't be protected from premium increases. The only exceptions are certain low-income individuals participating in special Part D subsidy programs.

This can mean hundreds of thousands of dollars in additional lifetime benefits, assuming you or your spouse lives many years beyond the break-even age. An individual who takes benefits at age 62 instead of 70 would receive $140,000 less in total lifetime benefits if that person or his spouse lived to age 90. And if the man or woman lives to age 95, then the loss is even higher—about $275,000. (The calculations assume an average Social Security benefit of $1,000 per month.)

Understanding Spousal Benefits

If you're married, it's crucial to understand the interaction of both spouses' benefits. Certain provisions of the Social Security law can create powerful amplifying effects when the higher-earning spouse waits to file for benefits until the NRA or beyond. The bottom line is that it's beneficial for the higher-earning spouse to delay taking Social Security benefits until the NRA or longer.

Spousal Benefit

As a spouse, you are entitled to receive the greater of your own benefit or half of your spouse's benefit. One strategy that isn't used very often—but is perfectly legal—is known as a *file-and-suspend*. Here's how it works:

1. The lower-earning spouse files for benefits at age 62.
2. The higher-earning spouse files for benefits at his or her NRA but immediately files a notice to suspend benefits.
3. The lower-earning spouse elects to receive spousal benefits (half of the higher-earning spouse's benefit).
4. The higher-earning spouse continues to accrue higher payments for whatever point he or she elects to begin receiving benefits.

Although this approach is kosher, it only makes sense if the spousal benefit would be higher than the individual's own benefit. The result can be much higher combined lifetime benefits for the couple.

Survivor Benefit

When a spouse dies, the survivor is entitled to receive the greater of his or her own benefit or 100 percent of the spouse's benefit, including any cost-of-living increases earned along the way. Again, if the higher-earning spouse delays filing until the NRA or beyond, then the surviving spouse's lifetime benefits will be increased substantially.

Maximizing the survivor benefit is an especially important consideration for women. Men not only tend to be the higher wage earners but also tend to die at younger ages than women. In many cases, this means that a delayed filing by a man can be a critical way to boost lifetime retirement security for older women—a time of life when overall income can decline sharply. In 2007, Social Security provided 90 percent or more of income for 47 percent of all elderly unmarried women who were receiving benefits.[10]

Social Security and Women

The income gap between working men and women is well known. But did you know that it spills over into retirement? Elderly women make up the largest segment of Americans living in poverty. For many of them, Social Security is a real lifesaver.

The gender gap in retirement income security is appallingly wide for several reasons. First, women earn about one-third less than men make during their working lives, which means they generate smaller contributions to Social Security, pension, and 401(k) benefit accounts. A contributing factor there is caregiving; women are far more likely to interrupt their working lives—or retire early—to take care of children or aging parents. That work most often is unpaid, so it interrupts and reduces employment and earnings.

Women also live longer than men. At age 65, a woman can expect to live an average of 19 more years—3 years longer than men. That means whatever a woman has saved for retirement must last longer.

The result is a yawning retirement security gap. In 2007, 20.5 percent of unmarried women ages 65 and older had income below 100 percent of the federal government's definition of poverty—far higher than rates experienced by men or married couples, according to Census Bureau data.

Cindy Hounsell has some ideas about improving this grim situation. She is executive director for the Women's Institute for a Secure Retirement (WISER), a not-for-profit group that works to promote financial education and planning among low- and moderate-income women. The group focuses on helping women take financial control over their lives and improve their retirement-income security.

When Hounsell counsels women, she always starts with Social Security. She advises women to pay close attention to the annual statement that we all receive each year projecting future Social Security benefits. "It's a day of reckoning," she says. "If that statement says you're going to get $1,000 a month, that's $12,000 a year. If you need $25,000 a year to live, there's your shortfall—and you need to do something about it."

Hounsell also believes women need to take more time to understand money and family finances. Many also don't focus on estimating what they'll really need in retirement—and don't get information and advice early enough in life to affect their retirement security.

A video interview with WISER Executive Director Cindy Hounsell on the financial issues women face in retirement can be viewed at http://retirementrevised.com/hounsell.

Paying Attention

Social Security sends you a birthday greeting every year around the time of your birthday—it's an annual statement estimating the benefits you and your family are entitled to. If you're like me, you don't pay much attention—but you should. Social Security will play a key role in your retirement security, so it's worth knowing more about the program and what you're likely to receive.

The Social Security Administration also has a useful Web site that can help with planning and the application process.

Resources

Applying for Social Security

Online. The Social Security Administration recently introduced an easy online application process at https://secure.ssa.gov/apps6z/iRRet/rib.

By phone. The toll-free number, open during regular business hours, is 1-800-772-1213 (TTY number, 1-800-325-0778).

In person. Social Security maintains an extensive network of local offices around the country, and you can apply in person. Call the toll-free number above to find your local office or find it online at https://secure .ssa.gov/apps6z/FOLO/fo001.jsp.

Documents. Social Security may require documents such as your Social Security card or number, a birth certificate, and proof of citizenship. In some cases, you may need to show military discharge papers if you served before 1968, a W-2 form from the previous year, or a tax return from the previous year if you are self-employed.

Estimating Your Benefits

Social Security estimator. The Social Security Administration offers a useful online retirement estimator (at www.socialsecurity.gov/estimator/) that allows you to project your future benefits assuming different retirement ages. The tool is free and easy to use: Just plug in basic personal data and your Social Security number; the site digs through your actual lifetime earning history and calculates your monthly benefit assuming different retirement ages. It's a useful decision-making tool and takes less than five minutes to use.

Social Security tables. The Social Security Administration publishes tables that show how much your benefits will be reduced under varying monthly benefit assumptions. Go to www.ssa.gov/retire2/ agereduction.htm.

Further Reading

The Social Security Fix-It Book. A concise, highly readable guide to the issues confronting Social Security and potential solutions is available from the Center for Retirement Research at Boston College. Download the guide here (http://crr.bc.edu/special_projects/the_social_ security_fix-it_book.html) or learn more about where a hard copy can be purchased.

Chapter Notes

1. Alicia H. Munnell, Francesca Golub-Sass, and Dan Muldoon, *An Update on 401(k) Plans: Insights from the 2007 SCF* (Chestnut Hill, MA: Center for Retirement Research at Boston College, March 2009).

2. Employee Benefit Research Institute, *Income of the Elderly Population Age 65 and Over, 2007, Notes* (May 2009), p. 9 (www.ebri.org/publications/notes/index.cfm?fa=notesDisp&content_id=4258), accessed June 2009.

3. Selena Caldera, "Social Security: Ten Facts That Matter" (Washington, DC: AARP Public Policy Institute, April 2009).

4. Caldera.

5. National Academy of Social Insurance, *Social Security: An Essential Asset and Insurance Protection for All* (Washington, DC: National Academy of Social Insurance, 2008), p. 5.

6. National Academy of Social Insurance, p. 5.

7. Social Security Administration, "Historical Background and Development of Social Security" (www.ssa.gov/history/briefhistory3.html), accessed June 2009.

8. National Academy of Social Insurance, p. 14.

9. Steven Sass, Alicia H. Munnell, and Andrew Eschtruth, *The Social Security Fix-It Book: A Citizen's Guide* (Chestnut Hill, MA: Center for Retirement Research at Boston College, 2007).

10. Social Security Administration, "Social Security Is Important to Women" (www.socialsecurity.gov/pressoffice/factsheets/women.htm), accessed July 2009.

CHAPTER 4

The Old-Fashioned Pension on Life Support

SOCIAL SECURITY AND A PENSION—there was a time when they went together like coffee and cream. As recently as 1980, 38 percent of private-sector American workers had traditional pension plans—funded and managed by employers and providing regular lifetime checks after retirement. By 2008, only 20 percent of workers had a defined benefit pension,[1] although greater percentages of large companies still offer them. And the recession has produced a steady stream of newspaper stories about troubled companies with endangered pension plans threatening the retirement of employees.

Traditional pensions are still common in the public sector, although chronic underfunding of plans by government employers—along with the use of accounting tricks to paper over problems—has created huge shortfalls in the amount of assets needed to cover the pension obligations of many plans. Overall, public pensions were underfunded by about 30 percent at the end of 2008; in some cases, the shortfalls are being covered by government borrowing, but that solution can't continue indefinitely. The likely result will be increased pressure to negotiate cuts in future benefits.

Although defined benefit (DB) pensions are waning, they're still a very big part of the American retirement-security system. DB plans don't seem likely to stage a big comeback in the private sector anytime soon, although some retirement-policy experts have started pushing for a publicly sponsored system with traditional pension features. One proposal calls for government-sponsored individual savings accounts that would guarantee a certain rate of return and include an annuity feature. Another—the automatic individual retirement account—would create a new system that encourages lower-income workers to save, coupling it with a series of simple investment choices.

If you do have a defined benefit pension, then you're in luck. It's one of the most automatic and reliable retirement benefits around, and it can be a critical income source in retirement.

Where the Pensions Are

Although defined benefit pensions have been on the decline, the percentages of companies offering them varies a great deal by industry. Employee-benefits consulting firm Watson Wyatt tracks pension benefits by sector; **Table 4.1** shows a breakout of traditional defined benefit plans, hybrid plans (usually, cash-balance), and defined contribution programs such as 401(k)s.

Table 4.1 Pensions in the Private Sector

Sector/Number of Employees	Pension (%)	Hybrid (%)	Defined Contribution Only (%)
Fortune 100 companies	22	23	55
5,000+ employees	27	21	53
Manufacturing: 1,000+	23	14	63
Nonmanufacturing: 1,000+	13	6	81
Finance: 1,000+	25	22	53
Health care: 1,000+	32	24	44
High tech: 1,000+	8	8	83
Telecommunications: 1,000	15	8	77
Energy, chemicals, pharmaceuticals: 1,000+	35	33	32
Retail: 1,000+	10	10	81

Source: 2007/2008 Watson Wyatt COMPARISON Database, reprinted with permission.

Safety

DB pensions have generated a good deal of bad press lately. A series of catastrophic, high-profile failures of big plans at companies such as United Airlines, US Airways, and Bethlehem Steel led to a series of sweeping reforms under the Pension Protection Act of 2006 (PPA), which required all private-sector plan sponsors to bring their plans to 100 percent funding levels over a period of years. The Great Recession all but guarantees more headlines about failed plans.

But here's the most important thing to know: If you work in the private sector and have a DB plan, it's probably backed by the Pension Benefit Guaranty Corporation (PBGC), a federally sponsored agency funded by insurance premiums paid by plan sponsors. The PBGC insures nearly

Tracking Your Pension

A defined benefit pension is one of your most important resources for retirement security. If you have one, keep tabs on how it's doing. The Pension Rights Center—a not-for-profit consumer group focused on retirement security—offers the following tips for monitoring your pension.

While You Are Working

➤ Keep records of your employment history as well as all correspondence, notices, and documents relating to the retirement plan and your benefits.

➤ Find out the rules of your plan by reading a copy of the summary plan description that is provided by employers.

➤ Verify the accuracy of the individual benefit statements you receive.

➤ Ask your plan administrator if there are restrictions on your ability to work after you start collecting your retirement benefits. Find out if part of your Social Security benefits will be subtracted from your pension.

➤ Check on your plan's funding status by reviewing the annual funding notice. You can also request the financial form that the plan files with the government each year (Form 5500).

➤ Contact your plan administrator to find out if your plan provides cost-of-living adjustments for pensioners.

If You Leave an Employer before Retirement Age

➤ Before leaving an employer, verify your current vesting status and your spousal or other beneficiary election.

➤ Before you leave, make sure you have a copy of the pension plan's most recent summary plan description (the one that is in effect on your last day of service).

➤ Keep track of your former employer. Corporate mergers, company relocations, bankruptcies, and plan terminations can make it harder for you to find your pension plan once you reach retirement age.

➤ Make sure your former employers or the pension plan administrators know how to contact you about your benefits.

When You Retire

➤ Generally, you must apply for benefits in order to begin receiving your pension.

➤ Read any and all forms you are asked to sign very carefully. Your choices cannot be changed after you retire.

➤ When you reach retirement age, check the accuracy of your company's benefit calculation. If the company's calculation seems incorrect, then immediately contact the plan administrator.

If Your Plan Is Terminated

➤ If your pension plan is terminated, find out who will be administering the pension plan and get the person's or agency's contact information from your former employer.

all private-sector plans; the main exceptions are professional-service employers such as physicians and lawyers as well as religious organizations. It does not cover public-sector employers.

When a plan covered by the PBGC fails, the agency takes over the responsibility to pay benefits up to an established maximum amount. Although it's possible to lose some income if your benefits exceed the PBGC's cap, most beneficiaries come out whole. For example, in 2009, workers who retired at age 65 could receive as much as $4,500 per month; the guaranteed amount is a bit lower for workers who retired at a younger age.[2]

The 2006 federal pension reforms also include important measures that protect pensions, including rules that mandate that all private-sector plans get to 100 percent funding of their liabilities over a seven-year period via increased contributions or improved investment performance. The PPA also improved the transparency of disclosures that employers must make to plan participants, requiring delivery of an "annual funding notice" that reports on the fund's financial condition and a variety of other details. The first reports under the new rules were distributed to beneficiaries in 2009.

Plan Sponsor Types

Plan sponsors for traditional defined benefit pensions generally fall into one of two categories:

Single employer. Single-employer plans are provided by a single plan sponsor; they are sometimes governed by collective-bargaining agreements.

Multiple employer. Multiple-employer plans are bargained collectively by a group of companies and a union, typically in large industrial businesses such as the automotive industry, trucking, and mining.

Benefit Types

Lifetime annuity. The lifetime annuity is the traditional DB plan. It offers a lifetime payment to the beneficiary and often to a surviving spouse. The benefit is sometimes expressed as a specific dollar amount per month for each year of employment at retirement, or it can be given as a formula based on a percentage of compensation (for each year of employment). The dollar amounts usually are fixed—that is, they are not adjusted for inflation after employment ends.

Cash balance. Cash-balance plans are hybrid defined benefit plans and are generally described to beneficiaries as having a hypothetical balance that is similar to what you'd see in a 401(k) plan. With these plans, workers accumulate credits based on a percentage of compensation as well as interest credits that typically are tied to U.S. Treasury security rates. But unlike 401(k) plans—which offer a defined employer *contribution* (typically based on a matching formula tied to the employee's contributions)—cash-balance plans are still defined *benefit* plans. That means the employer still has an obligation to pay out a specific sum, and the plans are guaranteed by the PBGC just like a traditional lifetime-annuity plan.

Cash-balance plans took off quickly in the mid-1980s, much as 401(k) plans did. Their adoption was slowed, however, by a lack of regulatory recognition of this type of design before passage of the PPA; it remains to be seen how they will fare going forward. Cash-balance plans do offer some advantages over traditional plans. They're more portable for workers who change jobs, and some people find them easier to understand because benefits are expressed in terms of a current value or account rather than a pension that is paid out on a regular basis, like an annuity.

What You'll Get and When

Defined benefit plans use formulas to determine benefits—for example, $10 per month for every year of service with an employer or a percentage of average salary at retirement multiplied by years of service.[3] Payments also are affected by age at retirement. In some cases, plans are integrated with Social Security payments—that is, the amount of payment is reduced by the amount of your estimated Social Security benefits.

Your date of retirement will affect payments, too. All plans have a defined normal retirement age tied to receipt of full benefits; by law, it can't generally be any later than age 65. Most plans include the option of survivor benefits for spouses, unless a couple has specifically declined that option in writing. It's worth noting that this option isn't free; the benefit paid to the employee is reduced to cover the cost of the survivor benefit.

Lump Sums Versus Lifetime Payout

For most people, a DB pension means a lifetime of benefit payments. But some pension recipients will have a choice at retirement between lifetime-annuity–style payments or a single lump sum that's calculated using longevity and interest-rate statistics. (About 30 percent of traditional DB participants have that option, and the percentage is much higher for hybrid-plan participants.)

You may be tempted by the large numbers involved to take a lump sum. Your financial adviser may also favor this approach, especially

Lump Sum? Avoid the Temptation

Why are lump sum payouts generally a bad option for DB participants? The answer is based on a series of actuarial assumptions, so let's get the answer from an actuary, Steve Verron, of Rest-of-Life Communications:

Let's assume that you're retiring at age 65, and have earned a monthly pension of $1,000, payable for your life. Using conversion factors that are in effect for 2009 for many pension plans, you would be offered a lump sum of roughly $140,000. For most people, that sounds like a lot more money than $1,000 per month. But is it?

If you elect a monthly annuity payment, it's pretty simple. You get $1,000 per month until you die, no matter how long you live, in good markets or bad. If you want to continue income to your spouse after you die, you can elect a joint and survivor income, with a lower monthly income. In the above example, if you have a 65-year-old spouse, you could elect to receive about $850 per month until the last one dies.

Instead, suppose you elect the lump sum. Now you need to invest this money to generate retirement income for the rest of your life, no matter how long you live. Suppose you think, "I could have received $1,000 per month with the annuity, so I'll take the lump sum and withdraw $1,000 per month." With this strategy, what are the odds of running out of money before you die (a.k.a. the odds of ruin)? It depends on a number of factors—how you invest the money, whether you're a male or female, and whether you're married.

If you invest in a diversified portfolio of stocks and bonds, the odds of ruin due to bad investment decisions are a little more than one in four for a single man, and a little more than one in three for a single woman. If you're a married couple and withdraw $850 per month, the odds are a little more than one in three that one of you will outlive your money.

The odds get much worse if you invest with an unscrupulous or incompetent adviser. The odds also get worse if you're healthier than average. Lump sums are based on the assumption that you will have average life expectancy, so if you're healthier than average, you're shooting yourself in the foot.[4]

if she's compensated based on the amount of your money under her management and has a focus on investing rather than on lifetime income. But you're almost always better off annuitizing your benefit over a lifetime. As we saw in Chapter 3, one of the most important keys to retirement security is *guaranteed income*. Both Social Security and income annuities provide that; a DB pension is your other opportunity to shore up long-term financial security significantly— but only if you elect regular lifetime payments. You're much more likely to come out ahead this way rather than trying to manage and invest a lump sum for maximum return.

The annuity option is one of the key benefits of defined benefit plans: They don't focus solely on accumulating funds during your working years. "One of the most important things about defined benefit plans is that they can help with planning for your retirement when you are in the spending phase of life," says Alan Glickstein, a senior consultant and pensions expert at Watson Wyatt, the big employee-benefits consulting firm. "You have the option to receive your benefit as a lifetime annuity. Most 401(k) plans don't do that."

A growing number of employers are offering the option of a retirement annuity as part of their workplace plans. And workplace annuity programs could get a further boost from the Obama administration, which is considering ways to improve guaranteed sources of retirement income.

Resources

U.S. Department of Labor

The online publication *What You Should Know about Your Pension Plan* (at www.dol.gov/ebsa/publications/wyskapr.html) provides an overview of all pension types regulated under federal law and includes a free downloadable PDF booklet.

"FAQs About Cash Balance Pension Plans" (at www.dol.gov/ebsa/FAQs/faq_consumer_cashbalanceplans.html) offers information on cash-balance pension plans as well as an overview of hybrid cash-balance defined benefit pensions.

Pension Rights Center

"How Well-Funded is Your Pension Plan?" The Pension Rights Center is a not-for-profit consumer organization that focuses on protecting and promoting retirement security. This online page (at www.pensionrights.org/pubs/facts/how-well-funded.html) explains how you can request specific information from your employer that details the health of your pension plan.

Pension Benefit Guaranty Corporation

The PBGC is the federally sponsored agency that insures private-sector pension plans. *A Predictable, Secure Pension for Life* (at www.pbgc.gov/docs/a_predictable_secure_pension_for_life.pdf) is a downloadable PDF guide to defined benefit pensions.

Rest-of-Life Communications

Steve Vernon is a former Watson Wyatt consultant and actuary with expertise in pensions, annuities, and Social Security. Rest-of-Life Communications (www.restoflife.com/) publishes educational DVDs, articles, and books on an array of retirement-security topics, including pensions.

Chapter Notes

1. Barbara A. Butrica, Howard M. Iams, Karen E. Smith, and Eric J. Toder. *The Disappearing Defined Benefit Pension and Its Potential Impact on the Retirement Incomes of Boomers* (Chestnut Hill, MA: The Urban Institute, January 2009), p. 5.

2. Pension Benefit Guaranty Corporation, Mission Statement (www .pbgc.gov/about/about.html), accessed July 2009.

3. Pension Benefit Guaranty Corporation, *A Predictable, Secure Pension for Life* (www.pbgc.gov/docs/a_predictable_secure_pension _for_life.pdf), accessed July 2009.

4. Based on an interview with Steve Vernon of Rest-of-Life Communications.

CHAPTER 5

Income Annuities
Another Way to Get
a Guarantee

LET'S SAY YOU WON'T have a defined benefit (DB) pension, or you expect a small pension that won't pay much. One option is to create a do-it-yourself pension. This is better known as an *income annuity*.

An income annuity is something like the mirror opposite of life insurance. A life insurance policy protects you and your family from the possibility you'll die prematurely; an income annuity insures you against the risk that you might outlive your assets.

The annuity market includes an almost dizzying array of products, but our main focus here will be on income annuities. The proposition is fairly simple: You make a payment to an insurance company, which in turn promises to send you a regular check starting on a specific date. In most cases, the payments continue so long as you live.

Income annuities aren't very popular as financial tools for retirement; private annuities represent only about 2 percent of total household income for current retirees.[1] People seem to have an overwhelming urge to take lump-sum payments over an income-annuity stream. When employer-sponsored retirement plans offer the choice of a lifetime annuity or a lump-sum payment, most employees choose the lump sum.[2] Estate and inheritance concerns are another reason income annuities haven't gained a lot of traction, because payments end when you die. Another problem holding back the annuity market is a lack of transparency. There's no widely accepted third-party source of information and ratings for consumers like the ones that exist for mutual funds—Morningstar, for example.

Some financial advisers aren't crazy about them either. In some cases, this is because their own performance and incentive compensation is geared to the total assets they manage: stocks, mutual funds, bonds, and the like. If a client spends $100,000 with an insurance company on an annuity, then those dollars disappear from the adviser's ledger. (That's one reason it makes so much sense to work with financial advisers who charge hourly or project fees rather than a percentage of assets under management; see Chapter 10.)

But the key point of hesitation for most people is simply this: They don't want to lose control of their assets. "When you look at all the studies on this, the main reason people don't buy an annuity is the 'wealth illusion,'" says Dallas Salisbury, president and chief executive officer of the Employee Benefit Research Institute. "A typical individual who is retiring with an accumulation of funds in a retirement plan is looking at a lump-sum payment that is more money than they have ever had in their life. If that person is told he can have this much at once or get a $300 monthly payment for life, that person almost always takes the lump sum—even though he would typically receive much more over the course of his life taking the $300 monthly payment."

An income annuity isn't a complete answer to your retirement income needs, but it can effectively address several key retirement-security issues. Here are some key reasons why income annuities are worth considering and why they should play a much larger role in providing retirement security than they have to date.

The Role of an Income Annuity

Cover the basics for life.   An income annuity can help cover basic living expenses beyond what you receive from Social Security or DB pension payments. The key here is that you're insuring yourself against so-called longevity risk—the danger that you could outlive your assets *or* that you'll spend less than you might have during retirement out of *fear* that you'll run out of money. With an annuity, you gain the certainty that no matter what else happens, you'll have the money you need for food, shelter, and other basics.

Longevity risk is a serious matter for many Americans, especially for women. The average life expectancy for a 65-year-old man is 17 years (82 years of age); it's 20 years for women (85 years of age).[3] And those figures are just averages, which means half of us will live *well beyond those ages.* An annuity that includes a joint and survivor provision can effectively cover you and your spouse for that risk.

Flexibility. An annuity gives you the freedom to take a more flexible approach in managing your other investments. Using an annuity to meet basic expenses can reduce the pressure to cash out equity holdings that have lost significant value, giving you a longer period of time for those assets to recover. Just as important, an annuity reduces the pressure you may feel to keep more of your portfolio invested aggressively to provide lifelong income.

Simplicity. "I've seen cases of dementia when people reach their 80s and 90s and really can't manage their money anymore," says Steve Vernon, an actuary and president of Rest-of-Life Communications. "At that point, it's really nice to have the simplicity of an electronic deposit to your checking account that comes like clockwork every month along with your Social Security check."

Sorting Out the Annuity Market

The overall annuity market can be confusing because insurance companies sell so many different product variations. But annuities boil down to two basic flavors: income annuities and deferred annuities.

Income annuities. An income annuity is a product you buy on retirement or later that is designed to start paying you a monthly sum right away. It's designed for the decumulation phase of life, so don't confuse it with deferred annuities, which are accumulation-phase products designed to earn an investment return. The most basic form is a single-premium immediate annuity (SPIA): You make a single payment up front to the insurance company and begin receiving payments immediately. The payment level depends on factors such as your age at the time of purchase, gender (women tend to live longer, so pricing will be a bit higher for them), survivor benefits, and whether you want the payments to last for a fixed period of time or the rest of your life. Two other important variables affecting premium price are whether you want joint and survivor benefits for your spouse and inflation riders that protect you against future cost-of-living increases.

Deferred annuities. Deferred annuities are designed for the accumulation phase of life; they help you accumulate funds in the years leading up to retirement for future payment. The investment earnings are tax sheltered until you withdraw funds, so insurance companies often pitch them as a way to save for retirement. However, deferred annuities typically are built on investment portfolios that include stocks and mutual funds that have variable rates of return. They may make sense in some situations, but they're not really very relevant to our task here—which is to identify straightforward ways to enhance financial security in a retirement that could last 25 years or more.

Moreover, when you buy an SPIA from an insurance company, you're getting the product that an insurance company is really good at making and selling. "Insurance companies are good at managing bond portfolios and real estate, and then turning around and promising you a fixed monthly income from those investments," says Steve Vernon. "These products have been around a long time, they're fairly efficient, and pricing is pretty good."

The rest of this chapter focuses on the ins and outs of income annuities.

How Much Should You Annuitize?

In Chapter 2, we talked about projecting your retirement income needs. If you've got that figured out, here's an easy way to think about the role of an annuity. Start with your total monthly expenses and subtract your expected Social Security and any other guaranteed income source such as a defined benefit pension. The *gap amount* is what you could fill with an income annuity.

Let's take as an example a 55-year-old man who earns $80,000 a year and hopes to replace 80 percent of that income at his planned retirement age of 66: $64,000, or $5,333 per month. For a very rough, back-of-the envelope illustration, let's assume a bit of additional income from part-time work. At retirement, the income equation stacks up as in **Table 5.1**.

Prices for annuities fluctuate, but a good ballpark figure for a single-premium annuity with no survivor benefits for our retiree is $184,000, according to ImmediateAnnuities.com, a website that allows you to do comparison shopping for policies. Changing that annuity to a joint life

Table 5.1 The Income Equation at Retirement

Monthly income target	$5,333
Social Security/month	3,039
Part-time income/month	1,000
Total income/month	4,039
Gap amount to annuitize	**$1,294**

policy that would continue paying benefits to his spouse after his death would increase the price to about $227,000.

Income-Annuity Options

The market for income-annuity products isn't terribly complicated, but there are several variations and options worth knowing about, and I detail them in **Figure 5.1**.

Some experts advise shopping for annuities with the help of a financial adviser who knows the market. Financial advisers may not be

Figure 5.1 Income-Annuity Types

➤ **Lifetime income:** Pays income for the rest of your life and then payments cease.

➤ **Life with period certain:** Pays income for the rest of your life. If you die before the "period certain" (often 10 years), your beneficiary receives the balance.

➤ **Life with refund certain:** Pays income for the rest of your life. If you die before you receive the amount paid in, your beneficiary receives the balance of the amount paid in.

➤ **Joint and survivor:** Lifetime income for two people. At the death of one person, the survivor receives a percentage of the original amount—for example, 50 percent or 100 percent.

➤ **Inflation:** Cost-of-living feature that provides automatic increases in payments indexed to inflation.

Source: Women's Institute for a Secure Retirement.

thrilled about getting you into an annuity for the reasons stated earlier, but they'll do so if you hold firm. If you use a fee-only adviser who isn't compensated from commissions on policy sales, then this can be a good way to assure yourself that you've shopped well. Moreover, working with your financial adviser is a good way to make sure your annuity is well integrated into your broader retirement plan. If you're comfortable shopping for an annuity on your own, use a Web site to help you to shop the market and get quotes, such as ImmediateAnnuities.com or Annuity.com.

Also check to see if your employer's benefit package includes an annuity-conversion option from your 401(k) plan on retirement; your employer may be able to get better group pricing than you'd find on your own and may already have done the hard work vetting carriers. However, don't opt for an employer plan without comparing annuity prices on your own.

A New Twist: Longevity Policies

If you expect to have enough income to support your basic needs but worry about longevity risk, the insurance industry offers another option you may want to consider.

A *longevity policy* is a deferred-annuity product that you buy when you're still relatively young; it starts generating payments to you only if you live to a certain age, typically 80 or 85. Many people have found the initial versions of longevity policies a tough proposition to swallow. You're buying a policy well in advance of the time you would need it—and you may never collect a dime. It's a relatively new product area, and only a handful of insurance companies offer these policies. But a longevity policy can give you certainty that you won't run out of money if you live a very long life, along with greater flexibility in the way you spend assets ahead of the date when the policy kicks in.

More recently, the insurance companies have been revising the way they bring these policies to market, stressing flexible options. When you compare these side by side, the payouts are very efficient from a tax standpoint because you're only taxed on the return of initial principal that you put into the policy. **Table 5.2**, provided by The Hartford insurance company, shows income-annuity choices that a 65-year-old couple could make, assuming they had $100,000 to invest and wanted a joint life policy with the option to receive some money back if circumstances change. The choices show payments beginning immediately and at increments of 5, 10, and 20 years in the future.

The payouts and rates of return start to look attractive—even eye-popping—the longer you defer, although the tax-free portion shrinks as the share of payment coming from investment returns rise. If you decide to pursue this route, a savvy financial planner can help you construct a laddered approach to the purchases to maximize tax efficiency.

Table 5.2 Income-Annuity Options: Immediate and Deferred

Income Start Date	Annual Payout ($)	Payout Rate (%)	Nonqualified Taxable Exclusions (%)
Immediate	6,600	6.60	59.60
5 years from issue	9,500	9.50	50.20
10 years from issue	14,900	14.90	39.80
20 years from issue	51,700	51.70	20.00

Source: Modified from The Hartford; reprinted with permission.

Safety

An income annuity is a promise from an insurance company to make payments to you over a long period of time, so the company's financial health is a major factor to consider when you shop. Be sure to buy from companies carrying top ratings from agencies such as A.M. Best, Moody's Investors Service, or the Standard & Poor's Insurance Ratings Service. Some experts also advise splitting your annuity income need among two or three policies from different carriers in order to spread the risk. But don't be overwhelmed by the possibility that your insurance company could fail. All legitimate insurance annuities are sold by licensed agents, and they are regulated by state insurance boards.

Contracts are backed by state guarantee associations that are funded by the insurance companies. Conditions for these guarantees vary by state, so check with regulators in your state for details.

Taxes

The IRS considers that your monthly check from the insurance company has two parts: (1) the return of principal, which isn't taxed because you've already paid taxes on the principal that you invest; and (2) the interest on the principal, which hasn't been taxed. You will pay income taxes on the portion of annuity payments that represent interest payments. Your insurance company will issue a federal 1099 tax statement annually indicating the portion of your annuity income that is taxable. That's how it works if you buy an annuity outside a tax-qualified retirement plan or individual retirement account.

Another option is to do the equivalent of a rollover with an account in a tax-qualified plan to buy your annuity. In that case, the money just goes directly from your 401(k) account to the insurance company. In this case, your account won't be taxed at the time of purchase, just like an IRA rollover. However, the entire monthly payment is taxed as ordinary income for the year in which you receive the income. Once again, the insurance company will issue the appropriate tax statements each year.

Chapter Notes

1. William G. Gale, J. Mark Iwry, David C. John, and Lina Walker, *Increasing Annuitization in 401(k) Plans with Automatic Trial Income* (Philadelphia: The Pew Charitable Trusts, Retirement Security Project, 2008) (www.pewtrusts.org/our_work_report_detail .aspx?id=40238&category=178), accessed June 2009.

2. Vanguard Center for Retirement Research, *The Retirement Income Landscape* (Valley Forge, PA: The Vanguard Group, December 2008) (https://institutional.vanguard.com/VGApp/iip/site/institutional/ researchcommentary/article?File=RetResRetireStrat), accessed June 2009.

3. Employee Benefit Research Institute, "Choose to Save" (Washington, DC: Employee Benefit Research Institute's Education and Research Fund, 2009) (www.choosetosave.org/calculators/index .cfm?fa=retireeCalc), accessed June 2009.

CHAPTER 6

Resuscitating the 401(k)

REMEMBER THAT OLD AD SLOGAN "When E.F. Hutton talks, people listen"?

Before the market crashed, the world of retirement planning was something like that. Planning for retirement and managing investment portfolios seemed synonymous. IRAs and 401(k) accounts were paramount in building a secure retirement. When the market talked, people listened.

But in 2008, the major stock indexes plunged by about 40 percent from their peak, and the value of equities in retirement accounts fell by almost $4 trillion. The losses in 401(k)s and IRAs accounted for about $2 trillion of those losses.[1] The attentiveness of retirement savers was transformed into rage.

"Get the hell out of the market," one reader said in a comment posted on my blog at The Huffington Post. "It is nothing but manipulation by the hedge funders and big brokers. . . . They want everybody's money, down to the penny!" Wrote another: "This is what we worked all our lives for? Worked and saved . . . tried to do everything 'responsible' to care for ourselves in retirement? Little did we expect our money to be spilled out by the billions to those thieves who tore the country's economy apart."[2]

At the other end of the spectrum are market cheerleaders such as Jim Kramer of CNBC, who still thinks the world revolves around stocks. "The stock market is the country right now," Kramer said in a 2009 television interview. "This is where people's wealth is. This is their pension plans, their 401(k)s, their IRAs."[3]

The truth lies somewhere between the two extremes. Even with the market setbacks and volatile outlook, 401(k) and IRA products will continue to play an important role in the American retirement system. But it's also clear that the system of voluntary contributions to defined contribution (DC) retirement accounts hasn't generated the levels of retirement security we need. Even before the crash, a debate was under way about ways to improve the system, and that discussion has been gaining volume. Some argue that the system of defined contribution has failed and should be scrapped in favor of a Social Security–style, government-sponsored annuity program. Others advocate boosting participation rates by mandating that employers offer plans and automated employee participation.

What role should 401(k) or IRA investing have in your retirement-security playbook? What should you be doing now to manage through a volatile market? The answers vary somewhat depending on your age. Younger investors, who won't need to start drawing down funds for decades, can afford to be patient. But for anyone who's retired recently—or plans to retire in the next five to ten years—the questions are much more difficult. If you're in the latter group, there are some smart strategic options that can help protect your remaining nest egg, although they're not painless. The key is maintaining a long-term perspective because the goal here is to make sure your retirement savings last many years into the future. The question really isn't what your portfolio looks like today, but how you'll manage it over a retirement that could last 25 years or more.

How We Got Here

Although it feels as if 401(k)s have been around forever, they're a recent innovation. Until the early 1980s, if you had a workplace retirement benefit, it came in the form of a traditional defined benefit (DB) pension. The DB pension system didn't require any active management by individuals; employers made the contributions and managed the pension funds. You were enrolled automatically on your hire date; when you retired, you began receiving a regular check that lasted for life.

The 401(k) takes its name from a section of the Internal Revenue code that made the accounts possible (this designation applies to private-sector employers; a similar public-sector option is known as the 457 plan, and not-for-profit employees can participate in 403(b) programs). The initial intent was to offer taxpayers breaks on deferred income;[4] but plan sponsors soon realized they could use the provision to offer voluntary workplace savings plans using a pretax payroll deduction, and the 401(k) took off in the early 1980s.

Initially, policy makers saw 401(k)s as a way to supplement existing DB pensions—and that's why they gave employees so much control over decisions such as whether to participate, how much to contribute, what to invest in, and when to withdraw funds.[5] But employers began reducing their commitment to DB plans as they looked for ways to get more competitive in an increasingly global economy. They saw DC plans as a way to cut expense and long-term funding obligations associated with defined benefit plans. Over the years, the balance shifted decisively away from DB plans and toward DC plans—so called because the employer's *contribution* to the plan is defined rather than the benefit that will be paid out. Some argue that defined contribution plans are better suited to an economy featuring rapid job turnover; DB plans—which can't be rolled over—are most valuable to participants with long job tenure. By contrast, DC plans offer the benefit of portability when workers change jobs.

The shift has been dramatic. In 2007, 63 percent of workers were covered only by defined contribution plans—up from just 12 percent in 1983.[6] And 67 percent of workers who participate in an employer-based retirement plan consider their defined contribution plan to be their primary retirement account (see **Figure 6.1**).[7]

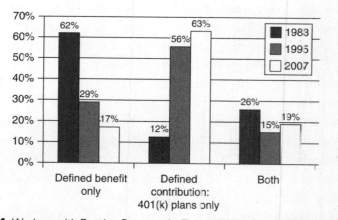

Figure 6.1 Workers with Pension Coverage by Type of Plan, 1983, 1995, and 2007

Note: Authors' calculations based on U.S. Board of Governors of the Federal Reserve System, *Survey of Consumer Finances* (SCF), 1983, 1995, and 2007.

Source: Center for Retirement Research at Boston College; reprinted with permission.

But DC pension plans have never come close to replacing DB plans as a source of retirement security—mainly because of inadequate participation by employers and employees alike and poor investment decisions by employees.

Access and participation. About 35 percent of American workers don't have access to a 401(k) plan at work; most work for smaller businesses that don't offer plans due to cost. Choice is another factor; 15 percent of workers who have access to a 401(k) decline to participate because they need the money for immediate expenses, or due to inertia. More than 70 percent of low-income households will reach retirement age without any employer-sponsored retirement coverage.[8]

Employer match. Although many employers match their employees' contributions, it's not mandatory. The recession prompted one-third of U.S. employers to cut or eliminate their matching contributions from the start of 2008 through April 2009, and another 29 percent told a pollster that they planned to do so.[9]

Low rates of saving. The average rate of employee contribution to 401(k) plans is 7.5 percent of salary;[10] that's about half the rate recommended by most financial planners.

Bad asset management. Apathy is a powerful force holding down 401(k) performance. The simple truth is that most people just don't want to be bothered managing their accounts and making investment decisions; only 19 percent of 401(k) plan participants make a trade of any kind in their accounts in a given year, according to Hewitt Associates, the employee benefits consulting firm. That lack of involvement—coupled with inadequate investment knowledge—often leads to an inappropriate portfolio mix. Nearly one in four investors approaching retirement age (56–65) had more than 90 percent of their account balances in equities at the end of 2007, and more than two in five had more than 70 percent in stocks.[11] That's far too high for older investors, who don't have nearly as much time as younger investors to recover from losses in a down market before the funds are needed.

Premature cash-outs. Account balances in 401(k)s grow most effectively over time, but about 45 percent of plan participants cash out their 401(k) balances when they change obs rather than roll them over to new employers or IRAs.[12] That disrupts the long-term growth of their assets. Borrowing and hardship withdrawals also are allowed under the rules, and people have been tapping into their balances somewhat more frequently during the economic crisis. The government tries to discourage this behavior by imposing a 10 percent penalty fee on withdrawals before age 59½. Borrowing from a 401(k) may seem like a good option if you are hard pressed by the economic crisis, but loans or withdrawals inflict serious damage on portfolios because you lose the opportunity to earn a return on the funds that are withdrawn. Also lost is the opportunity to earn returns on new investments; in most cases, you can't make contributions while you have a loan outstanding, and you can't contribute for six months after you make a hardship withdrawal.

All these trends add up to a simple fact: For too many Americans, 401(k) accounts simply haven't been getting the job done. In 2007—before the crash—the median amount saved by households headed by a person in the preretirement years (54–65) was $50,500.[13] Savings in 401(k)s and IRAs are a distant fourth after Social Security, the value of a primary home, and a defined benefit pension (for those lucky enough to have one) (see **Table 6.1**).

Table 6.1 Wealth of a Typical Household Approaching Retirement, 2007

Source of Wealth	Amount in Dollars	Percent of Total
Primary house	138,600	20
Business assets	15,900	2
Financial assets	29,600	4
401(k)/IRAs[a]	50,500	7
Defined benefit	122,100	18
Social Security	298,900	44
Other nonfinancial assets	21,000	3
Total	676,500	100

[a]Includes thrift savings plans and other defined contribution plans.

Notes: The "typical household approaching retirement" refers to the mean of the middle 10 percent of the sample of households headed by an individual aged 55–64.

Authors' calculations based on the 2007 SCF.

Source: Center for Retirement Research at Boston College; reprinted with permission.

Target Date Funds: Putting It on Cruise Control

Washington took steps to shore up retirement security with passage of the Pension Protection Act (PPA) of 2006—a broad set of reforms to defined benefit and defined contribution pensions. The bill was hardly a cure-all, but it did contain some important reforms. One of the most significant provisions cleared a path for plan sponsors to offer automated investment options called *target date* or *lifecycle retirement funds*. These funds provide a sort of cruise control to retirement investing. Instead of sorting through fund options in your employer's plan and making periodic adjustments, you simply pick a fund targeted for the year you expect to retire. The fund manager adjusts assets as the target year approaches, reducing the percentage of equities and increasing fixed-income investments to make the overall mix more conservative. The changes contained in the PPA led to a flood of new investment in these vehicles. Assets in target date funds rose 61 percent in 2007 to $183 billion, according to the Investment Company Institute; 88 percent of those assets was in retirement accounts. Assets in target date accounts were depressed in 2008 because of the market crash, but the number of plan sponsors offering them is continuing to grow quickly.

Here's the rub: The law doesn't set any definitions for appropriate equity-exposure levels by age group, so fund managers have been free to manage the investment mix as they see fit. As a result, target date funds have come under fire since the crash because many of the funds tailored for investors near retirement age racked up significant losses. Morningstar reported that target funds with dates between 2000 and 2010 lost 22.5 percent in 2008, and funds with target dates between 2011 and 2015 lost 28 percent.* But those are broad averages; some funds with dates as early as 2010 lost as much as 50 percent of their value in 2008.

Target date funds have helped eliminate some of the most extreme allocation imbalances: young investors who are badly underweight in stocks and older investors who are very overweight.**

But many of these funds have failed to meet expectations of older investors who thought they were buying more protection from market risk. The problem centers around the so-called glide path to retirement: the approach fund managers take to reduce exposure to equities or other riskier assets as the investor ages. Approaches here vary, but most of the big mutual fund–management companies argue that investors need to maintain a healthy amount of equity exposure to help insure against longevity risk. T. Rowe Price, for example, has an asset-allocation glide path that starts with 90 percent equity exposure for investors more than 25 years away from retirement; the exposure drops to 55 percent at age 65, 35 percent at age 80, and 25 percent at age 95 and thereafter.

A debate is under way among regulators and the fund industry about possible target date fund reforms, and at minimum it seems likely there will be a push for greater disclosure and investor education about what these funds really do. It's also possible—but less likely—that regulators will set standards for glide-path allocation. If you do use a target date fund, be sure to understand the glide-path strategy in the years near retirement and decide if you're comfortable with the equity exposure involved. If not, then you can fashion a more conservative investment mix and make plans to insure for longevity risk via another route—for example, an income annuity or deferred longevity policy (see Chapter 5).

Notes

* Eleanor Laise, "Target-Date Funds Come Under Fire," *Wall Street Journal* (June 19, 2009), p. C9.

** Jack VanDerhei, "The Impact of the Recent Financial Crisis on 401(k) Account Balances," *EBRI Issue Brief* (February 2009) (www.ebri.org/publications/ib/), accessed June 2009.

What Now?

How bad is the wreckage from the market crash? The Standard & Poor's (S&P) 500 Index lost 37 percent of its value in 2008 before the market began its recovery in 2009. But that's just a broad average; the actual impact on retirement savers varied depending on factors such as size of account, age, and job tenure.[14] Plan participants with

Automating the IRA

One of the toughest challenges facing our retirement-savings system is the simple fact that half of the country's working population doesn't have access to a workplace savings plan. One idea favored by the Obama administration would create a new retirement-savings vehicle called the *Automatic IRA*. The idea enjoys some bipartisan support. The account would serve as a sort of defined contribution cousin to the Social Security system.

The idea was hatched by the Retirement Security Project (RSP), a nonpartisan organization whose principals include experts from the mostly liberal Brookings Institution and the conservative Heritage Foundation. Companies that are not willing to sponsor any retirement plan, have been in business for more than two years, and have more than ten employees would be mandated to offer a payroll-deduction savings option to their employees—no different from the way employers deduct for taxes. Employees would be enrolled automatically when they are hired—unless they chose to opt out.

Although the word *mandate* often is used as a political weapon, the truth is that this plan would be fairly painless for employers. They wouldn't have to make matching contributions or comply with the qualification and fiduciary standards required in employer-sponsored plans. The employer simply acts as a conduit, remitting the deducted pay to an IRA.

Another RSP idea complements the Automatic IRA by changing the current savers' tax credit to make it refundable. The current rule offers a nonrefundable credit for as much as $2,000 for lower- and moderate-income married couples for contributions to an employer plan or IRA. But that has value only if you have an income-tax liability. The RSP plan would be refundable and added directly to the saver's retirement account, so it would help even those who owe no income tax.

The Automatic IRA would put savers in a default investment, such as a lifecycle fund geared to the individual's expected retirement age, with two or three simple alternative investment options for those who decided to opt out.

The RSP has also proposed that 401(k) plan sponsors be encouraged to automatically offer to convert at least some portion of each account into a simple annuity on retirement unless the saver specifically opts out. An estimated 50 million families could benefit from the RSP proposals.

The Obama administration got the ball rolling in this direction in the fall of 2009 with a series of policy charges aimed at encouraging retirement saving, including streamlining automatic-enrollment options in 401(k) plans that would make it easier for workers to automatically increase their contribution rates over time.

low account balances experienced smaller losses that tended to be made up for by continuing contributions. For example, people with less than $10,000 in their accounts actually saw an average growth of 40 percent in 2008. But participants with more than $200,000 had losses averaging more than 25 percent. Similarly, plan participants close to retirement age (56–65) had average changes in 2008 ranging from 1 percent gains for people invested in a plan from one to four years to 25 percent losses for those with long tenures (more than 20 years).

How long will it take for retirement investors to recoup their losses from the crash? The Employee Benefit Research Institute looked at how long it would take for 401(k) balances to recover from their levels at the end of 2008, assuming different rates of return. If the stock market generates 5 percent returns over the next few years, the median figure for recovery is two years; 90 percent of investors will have recovered five years out. On the other hand, if the market return is zero for the next few years, then the median recovery time lengthens to 2.5 years, with 90 percent of investors recovering within 9 or 10 years.[15]

No one knows what the market actually will do. But let's assume—as I do—that our struggling economy will produce subpar returns over the next three to five years. If that's the case, what strategies can you use to help mend your own account?

Younger Investors

If you're younger than 50, you've got time for the market to bounce back. The most effective strategy is to automate where you can, save steadily, and look into the possibility of a Roth IRA.

Automate. Make regular, automated contributions to your retirement account at work and use target date or index funds that put your portfolio on cruise control. Most investors don't have the time, patience, or knowledge to drive their own investing.

Keep saving. Most financial planners recommend that you save 15 percent of your pretax income if possible. Don't get distracted if your employer reduces or eliminates a matching contribution; a plan sponsor's decision to cut back a match is driven by decisions that have nothing to do with your own investing and saving.

Consider a Roth. With a Roth IRA, you can invest after-tax income up to a specified amount each year. Earnings on the account are tax free, and tax-free withdrawals can be made after age 59½. These features can boost the value of your holdings upon retirement. You can't contribute pretax dollars to a Roth IRA, but it has other key advantages:

➤ *Tax planning.* Withdrawals from tax-sheltered accounts are taxed as ordinary income, and that can have negative consequences for your overall tax situation in retirement because your bracket can be somewhat fluid after you stop working. Sometimes, taking a distribution from a tax-deferred account can put you into a higher bracket than you want to be in, boosting your tax bill. With a Roth IRA, you've paid the income tax up front because you invested post-tax dollars. That means your withdrawals are tax free so long as the account has been open five years and you are at least 59½ years old. Roths also can be a good tax hedge if you believe—as I do—that today's historically low federal income-tax rates are destined to rise in the years ahead. If you think taxes will be higher when you retire than they are today, you can use a Roth to pay the taxes at the current lower rates.

➤ *Flexible withdrawals.* Unlike traditional IRAs, no required minimum distribution is necessary with a Roth when you turn 70½. That gives you the potential to keep more of your money invested and working for you and boosting your long-term retirement security.

At or Near Retirement Age

The key here is maintaining a long-term perspective because the goal is to make sure your retirement nest egg lasts many years into the future. So the question isn't really what your portfolio looks like today, but how you'll manage it over what could be a retirement of 25 years or more.

T. Rowe Price has analyzed possible outcomes for investors who had the bad fortune to retire into a bear market. The investment-management company did a Monte Carlo probability analysis to determine which investment-management decisions would allow investors to make the most of their nest-egg savings over a 30-year retirement.

The analysis looked at 10,000 simulated portfolio outcomes using actual stock performance data from 2000 to 2002—a period in which the S&P 500 fell 42 percent. The analysis assumed a tax-deferred portfolio invested 55 percent in equities and 45 percent in bonds. The analysis underscores the importance of adjusting your strategy in a bear market—but not panicking.

The worst decision you can make. Sell off all your stocks at the market bottom and switch to a portfolio that holds only conservative, fixed-income investments such as bonds. With this emotion-driven approach, there is only a 5 percent chance that your retirement nest egg will last 30 years, according to the probability analysis. Not only do you suffer the losses of selling at the bottom but also, with all your money in bonds, you miss out on the growth from equity investments when the market rebounds, as well as all the successive rallies that follow in succeeding decades.

The best decision you can make. Don't sell. Instead, adjust your plans for withdrawing funds—especially in the early years of retirement. Most financial advisers recommend withdrawing 4 percent of a nest-egg balance in the first year of retirement and increasing annual withdrawals by 3 percent annually to keep pace with inflation. But in

Resisting the Urge to Raid Your 401(k)

In tough times, you may be tempted to raid your retirement account to meet current needs—and that's understandable. But this should be among the last financial options that you consider, not the first.

Government rules permit borrowing and hardship withdrawals from 401(k) accounts, and more than 85 percent of plan sponsors offer these options to workers. Borrowing from a 401(k) may seem attractive if your circumstances are dire. Since you're borrowing your own money, it's one of the easiest forms of credit you can qualify for. And the interest rate will be lower than some other forms of consumer debt—typically prime plus one or two points. But a 401(k) loan can spell short-term financial trouble and pose a threat to your retirement security.

Job change is one possible complication. These loans have five-year terms; if you leave your job for any reason before then, you must repay in full or the loan is treated as a taxable distribution. If you default on the loan and you're younger than 59½, you'll pay a 10 percent early-withdrawal penalty.

Hardship withdrawals have drawbacks, too. In most cases, you'll pay the 10 percent early-withdrawal fee if you are under 59½. The Internal Revenue Service only allows these withdrawals for limited and very specific purposes, including funding of medical expenses and funerals, paying mortgage debt, and avoiding foreclosure or eviction. The IRS requires employers to meet tough qualification requirements for approving hardship withdrawals, and employees must submit extensive documentation proving the hardship.

Borrowing or withdrawing funds will inflict serious damage because of the time those funds won't be earning investment returns. You also lose the opportunity to earn returns on new investments; in most cases, you can't make contributions while you have a loan outstanding, and you can't contribute for six months after you make a hardship withdrawal.

I asked the Transamerica Center for Retirement Studies to run some what-if scenarios demonstrating just how much damage can be done. We worked with the example of a 35-year-old investor who plans to retire at 65, contributes $5,000 a year to a 401(k) account, and has a current vested balance of $50.000. If the money is left untouched, then this investor would have $693,000 at retirement. Taking a $25,000 loan and repaying it over 5 years would reduce this investor's account total at retirement to $576,000—a loss of 17 percent. The most damage was done by a hardship withdrawal of $50,000; forced to start over with new contributions a year later, the investor would have just $378,000 at retirement—a whopping 45 percent reduction.

You can view the detailed scenario here: http://retirement revised.com/loanhardship.

one of T. Rowe Price's hypothetical scenarios, the retiree holds off taking any inflation adjustments for several years—until the market rebounds. That decision has a very positive impact on portfolio longevity; in fact, it yields an 89 percent probability that the retiree's funds will last 30 years (see **Figure 6.2**).

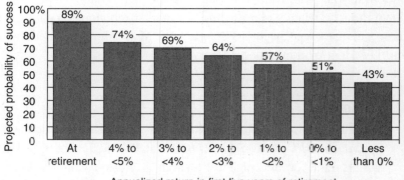

Annualized return in first five years of retirement

Figure 6.2 For Retirement Success, the First Five Years Are Critical

Note: This chart shows the probability of not running out of money over a 30-year retirement for an investor who withdraws 4 percent of her portfolio the first year and increases the annual withdrawal amount by 3 percent for inflation. If portfolio returns are weak in the first five years and the investor doesn't cut back on withdrawals, the likelihood of not running out of money can drop sharply from the 89 percent probability of success at the start of retirement.

Source: T. Rowe Price; reprinted with permission.

In a much more aggressive scenario, T. Rowe Price assumes that the hypothetical retiree reduces planned withdrawals by 25 percent. That restores a 99 percent probability that the funds will last 30 years—but it's too draconian a cut for most people. Still, it does illustrate the potential available to you in holding back on withdrawals. (One caveat: Because tax-deferred accounts require that you take minimum distributions starting at age 70½, T. Rowe Price assumed that these distributions aren't spent but are instead reinvested in taxable equity accounts.)

No doubt, these suggestions represent belt-tightening. After all, we're talking about weathering a tough market and recession. But remember: The main objective is to maintain your nest egg to support a long retirement. So the question here is, can you reduce your planned expenses enough to make the adjustments? T. Rowe Price Senior Financial Planner Christine Fahlund—who did the analysis—points out that cutting back on spending in early retirement is feasible for many. "It works best if you can start with discretionary items, especially big-ticket expenditures. Don't redo the kitchen, or don't buy a new car."

Also consider putting off retirement or going back to work, if that's an option. Working a few additional years will fatten your Social Security payments considerably, and every year you work is a year you won't be drawing down 401(k) balances. Instead, you'll be making payroll contributions to your plan. Those investments then have a chance of paying off down the road when you retire and the market rebounds. For more on these strategies, see Chapters 3 ("Getting the Most from Social Security") and 11 ("How Working Longer Helps").

Chapter Notes

1. Alicia H. Munnell, Francesca Golub-Sass, and Dan Muldoon, *An Update on 401(k) Plans: Insights from the 2007 SCF* (Chestnut Hill, MA: Center for Retirement Research at Boston College, March 2009).

2. Mark Miller, "A Kinder, Gentler Recession for Seniors?" The Huffington Post (June 3, 2009) (www.huffingtonpost.com/mark-miller/a-kinder-gentler-recessio_b_210057.html), accessed June 2009.

3. Mark Miller, "Is Wall Street Still America?" The Huffington Post (March 4, 2009) (www.huffingtonpost.com/mark-miller/is-wall-street-still-amer_b_171734.html), accessed June 2009.

4. Alyssa Fetini, "A Brief History of the 401(k)," *Time* (October 16, 2008) (www.time.com/time/printout/0,8816,1851124,00.html), accessed June 2009.

5. Munnell, Golub-Sass, and Muldoon.

6. Munnell, Golub-Sass, and Muldoon.

7. Jack VanDerhei, "The Impact of the Recent Financial Crisis on 401(k) Account Balances," *EBRI Issue Brief* (February 2009) (www.ebri.org/pdf/briefspdf/EBRI_IB_2-2009_Crisis-Impct.pdf), accessed June 2009.

8. Robert Stowe England, "Principles for a New Retirement System," *Retirement USA* (March 10, 2009), p. 5 (www.retirement-usa.org/wp-content/.../working-paper-031209.pdf.

9. Jeff Plungis, "More U.S. Employers Reducing 401(k) Match, Study Says," Bloomberg.com (March 25, 2009) (www.bloomberg.com/apps/news?pid=20601103&sid=ahfAY85xO2vw&refer=us), accessed June 2009.

10. Employee Benefit Research Institute, "Average Worker Contribution Rates to 401(k)-Type Plans" (March 2009) (www.ebri.org/pdf/FFE117.19March09.Final.pdf), accessed June 2009.

11. VanDerhei.

12. Munnell, Golub-Sass, and Muldoon.

13. Munnell, Golub-Sass, and Muldoon.

14. VanDerhei.

15. VanDerhei.

CHAPTER 7

Managing Your Health-Care Expense Burden

A GOOD FRIEND IS planning to throw herself a Medicare birthday party when she turns 65 a few years from now. She lost her employer-sponsored health insurance several years ago after retiring early, and has struggled along ever since with an individual insurance policy that features high deductibles and limited coverage. She thinks Medicare will solve all her health insurance problems.

It's true that Medicare is fairly comprehensive—and very popular with beneficiaries. But Medicare doesn't cover everything—long-term care, for example. And it's not a free lunch. You'll pay premiums to receive some Medicare benefits, such as physician services and drug benefits. Insurance premiums and out-of-pocket expenses will make health care one of your most significant expenses in retirement—and one that can pose a major threat to retirement security.

The nation's health-care system is in crisis; the recent national health-care reform debate focused attention on exploding costs, rising use of services, and a patchwork insurance system that leaves many Americans uncovered. The new reform law is good news—and not only for retired people. The crisis is especially acute for the uninsured, a group that includes a broad cut of the population across age groups. If you're age 65 or older, Medicare provides an important safety net. But there is a large and growing group of uninsured people in their fifties and early sixties who have been forcibly retired by the recession. Even for those on Medicare, out-of-pocket health-care expense is eroding spending power and economic security. Fidelity Investments has been publishing an annual report on retiree health-care expenses since 2002. In that time, average annual costs have jumped more than 50 percent, rising 4.2 percent since 2009. Fidelity reports that a 65-year-old couple retiring in 2010 will need to spend $250,000 in retirement to cover out-of-pocket medical expenses, assuming that the man lives 17 additional years and the woman 20. That includes premiums for Medicare and expenses outside Medicare, such as over-the-counter medications, dental care, and long-term care. Medicare premiums—which usually are deducted from Social Security benefits—currently consume 14 percent of Social Security checks, a figure that is projected to soar in the years ahead unless costs are reduced through reform measures.

That sounds like a lot of money—and it is. But what does it mean in the context of overall retirement security? The Center for Retirement Research (CRR) at Boston College created the National Retirement Risk Index (NRRI) to answer this question. *Risk* is defined as the likelihood that individuals will not be able to maintain their standard of living in retirement. Excluding health care, the NRRI shows that 44 percent of Americans are at risk; when health care is added, the number jumps to 61 percent. And those projections are conservative because they make some optimistic assumptions about how Americans will manage their money in the years ahead. As **Figure 7.1** shows, today's seniors and older

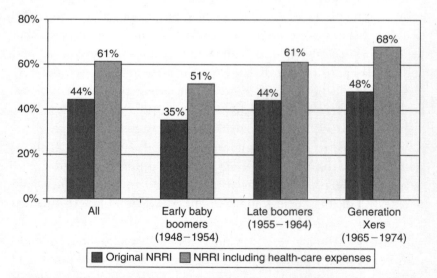

Figure 7.1 National Retirement Risk Index: How Health Care Affects Retirement Security

Source: Center for Retirement Research at Boston College; reprinted with permission.

baby boomers are somewhat less at risk than younger boomers and the members of Generation X because CRR's model assumes rising health-care cost over time and fewer available resources to pay for it by the time younger Americans reach retirement age.

All told, health care is one enormous wild card in the deck when it comes to retirement security. Even if you've been socking away money to pay for your health care, it's hard to know what you'll really need. How long will you live? What will be the quality of your health as you age?

Health-Care Risk: A Closer Look

Americans are living longer than ever. An American who lives to age 65 can expect to live an average of 18.7 years longer, or 7 years longer than a 65-year-old living in the year 1900.[1] But the additional years aren't necessarily healthy ones. Old age in the United States often is accompanied by disease and disorders, with large proportions of the older population experiencing chronic conditions such as hypertension, arthritis, and diabetes. So you're likely to need more health care as you age.

Health can pose another kind of retirement-security risk—what some experts call a health-care "shock"—that can derail your plans. Health problems often develop as people near retirement age, no matter how well they take care of themselves. A health-related disability that prompts premature retirement translates into lower pension benefits and a need to spread resources over more years than anticipated. And if medical trouble comes along at a time of joblessness, health insurance can be very difficult to get, and very expensive.

What can you do to mitigate health-care risk? Experts point to several concrete steps you can take—although none are easy.

➤ **Increase your savings.** Add health care to your overall calculation of retirement expenses; adjust your rate of saving accordingly.
➤ **Work longer.** Staying on the job even a few years longer than planned is one of this book's most important overall recommendations, and health insurance is one of the key reasons. Working longer makes it possible to save more, and it gives you more years of employer-sponsored health insurance. If full-time work isn't possible, try to stay on part-time if that will allow you to stay insured.

➤ **Adopt a healthier lifestyle.** It may sound like a mom-and-apple-pie suggestion, but increasing your exercise and losing weight will not only make you feel and look better but also help reduce your risk of diabetes and heart disease.

➤ **Practice prevention.** Make sure you get regular checkups and recommended screenings for diseases such as cancer—especially when you have insurance coverage.

➤ **Select quality hospitals.** Better outcomes from treatments and procedures mean fewer complications and lower risk of additional costs. You can compare the quality of care for specific hospitals, procedures, and surgeries using a database developed by the U.S. Department of Health and Human Services (see Resources at the end of this chapter).

➤ **Review your paperwork for errors.** The billing and claim process is complicated, and providers do make errors that can cost you money. Always review your paperwork carefully and don't hesitate to challenge or ask questions.

When You're 65: Welcome to Medicare

If you've ever wondered what it would be like to have a European-style, single-payer health-care system in the United States, consider Medicare. The federal government created the program in the 1960s to help older Americans who were having trouble finding affordable health-insurance policies. The program has solved that problem and then some; it's the largest health-insurance program in the United States and provides a basic safety net to every American age 65 or older. (If you file early for Social Security, you'll still wait until 65 for Medicare!) But Medicare doesn't cover everything—long-term care, for instance—and it has become more complicated over the years by the addition of an array of private add-on plans such as Medicare Advantage and Medicare D prescription-drug coverage, which are intended to fill the gaps and cap your out-of-pocket expenses.

The initiative to pass Medicare began with the 1960 election of President John F. Kennedy; as a candidate, he supported government-sponsored health insurance for older Americans. There were numerous political clashes in the ensuing years over the shape of the program. Organized labor and senior citizens' groups pushed for a comprehensive program that leveraged the existing Social Security program; the American Medical Association and Republicans opposed federal intervention in health care and proposed alternatives such as voluntary participation and a system of means-based qualification.[2]

The final Medicare bill signed into law in 1965 by President Lyndon Johnson was a compromise among the various approaches and laid the foundation for Medicare as we know it today. At the outset it provided coverage to 19 million Americans; today it covers 37 million age 65 and older and another 7 million people with disabilities.

Traditional Medicare (Parts A and B) provides basic health services but with some costs borne by beneficiaries through premiums and copayments. Unlike most private health-insurance plans, Medicare has no overall limit on out-of-pocket expenses—which means you face risk in cases of the most serious, care-intensive illness. Should you need long-term care, you're on your own. The basic program also doesn't cover dental expenses or over-the-counter medicines.

Enrollment in basic Medicare is automatic at age 65 *if* you already receive Social Security benefits. Your Medicare card will be mailed to you about three months before your eligible date. Otherwise you'll need to enroll.

Part A: Hospital Coverage

Medicare Part A covers stays at hospitals and skilled nursing facilities. When Medicare beneficiaries are hospitalized, they pay a deductible ($1,068 in 2009) that covers an initial period of care, with copayments required after that period (see **Table 7.1**).

Part B: Medical Coverage

Medicare Part B covers outpatient services, including physician and nursing services, tests, vaccinations, and a variety of therapies and other services (see **Table 7.2**). Medicare publishes a schedule of approved provider charges for various services, paying 80 percent of those rates. Patients pay the other 20 percent plus an annual deductible. You can go to any health provider that accepts Medicare. Doctors are permitted to charge more than the scheduled rates under certain circumstances, but beneficiaries can't be charged more than 15 percent above the scheduled

Table 7.1 Medicare Part A

Benefits	Individual Pays (in 2009)
Inpatient hospital	Deductible of $1,068 per benefit period[a]
Days 1–60	No coinsurance[b]
Days 61–90	$267 a day
Days 90–150	$534 a day
After 150 days	No benefits
Skilled nursing facility	
Days 1–20	No coinsurance
Days 21–100	$133 a day
After 100 days	No benefits
Home health	No deductible or coinsurance[b]
Hospice	Copayment of up to $5 for outpatient drugs and 5% coinsurance for inpatient respite care

[a] A benefit period begins when a person is admitted to a hospital and ends 60 days after discharge from a hospital or a skilled nursing facility. The deductible is the amount an individual must pay before Medicare begins to pay for services.

[b] Coinsurance: portion of a health-care fee that must be paid by an insured patient.

Source: "Talking About Medicare: Your Guide to Understanding the Program, 2009," The Henry J. Kaiser Family Foundation; reprinted with permission.

prices—although many physicians accept the Medicare reimbursement rate as payment in full.

How do we pay for all this? Part A is funded by a payroll tax of 1.45 percent on all wages and salaries (Federal Insurance Contributions Act, or FICA, taxes). Part B is funded by premiums, which usually are deducted from your Social Security benefits check. The premiums charged are adjusted according to your income—but not by much. In 2009, if your modified adjusted gross income (MAGI) was less than $85,000 a year (or $170,000 for married couples), then the premium was $96.40 per month per person; for beneficiaries with MAGI higher than those figures, the premium was somewhat higher, ranging from about $134 to $308 monthly. (For Medicare purposes, the federal government defines MAGI as a combination of your adjusted gross taxable income and tax-exempt interest income.)

That's traditional, basic Medicare. But many Americans supplement that with additional coverage. Some retirees are covered by health insurance provided by their employers; many others purchase supplemental insurance policies from private insurance companies

Table 7.2 Medicare Part B

Benefits	Individual Pays (in 2009)
Premium	$96.40[a]
Deductible	$135 a year
Physician and other medical services MD accepts assignment[d] MD does not accept assignment	20% coinsurance 20% coinsurance plus up to 15% over Medicare-approved fee[b]
Outpatient hospital care	20% coinsurance
Ambulatory surgical services	20% coinsurance
X-rays; durable medical equipment	20% coinsurance
Physical, speech, and occupational therapy	20% coinsurance[c]
Clinical diagnostic laboratory services	No coinsurance
Home health care	No coinsurance
Outpatient mental health services	50% coinsurance[e]
Preventive services - Flu shots; pneumococcal vaccines; colorectal cancer screenings; prostate cancer screenings; mammograms; Pap smears; pelvic exams	Part B deductible and 20% coinsurance waived for certain preventive services
- Bone mass measurement; diabetes monitoring; glaucoma screening	20% coinsurance

[a]Higher premiums (up to $308.30/month) for beneficiaries with higher incomes ($85,000/individual; $170,000/couple in 2009). Low-income individuals receiving Medicaid or Medicare Savings Program benefits do not pay monthly premiums.

[b]Referred to as the Medicare Limiting Charge Law, the limit on the percentage above the Medicare-approved amount that a physician can charge is less than 15% in some states.

[c]There is a coverage limit on Medicare outpatient therapy services. A $1,740 limit per year for occupational therapy services, and a $1,740 limit per year for physical and speech-language therapy services combined.

[d]Assignment: Physicians agree to accept Medicare's predetermined fee as payment in full; patients are responsible for 20% copayment but no more.

[e]Beginning in 2010, the coinsurance will phase down to 20%.

Source: "Talking About Medicare: Your Guide to Understanding the Program, 2009." The Henry J. Kaiser Family Foundation; reprinted with permission.

that protect them against potentially high out-of-pocket expenses. In addition, private plans are available for prescription drugs and dental or vision care.

Retiree coverage from employers once was commonplace, but it has become more rare. If you're lucky enough to have employer coverage, then Medicare is your primary payer if you already are retired, with the employer coverage filling gaps such as prescription drugs or capping out-of-pocket costs. Unfortunately, the number of employers providing retiree coverage has declined sharply; the percentage of large companies providing it fell from 66 percent in 1988 to just 31 percent in 2008.[3]

The Detroit automakers are the highest-profile example of this trend. Detroit once was the gold standard in employee benefits—the result of decades of collective bargaining with the United Auto Workers (UAW) union. As the industry's woes accelerated in recent years, the automakers have been wrangling with the UAW over their massive contractual obligations to provide retiree health coverage; in 2007 a deal was struck to spin off the retiree health plans into a stand-alone trust that would receive $60 billion in payments from the companies. It now appears that a good portion of those payments will come in the form of company stock, and observers give the trust poor odds of survival.

The growing sector of supplemental coverage is Medicare Advantage, or private Medicare plans that offer all-in-one medical and drug coverage. Participation has doubled to about 10 million since 2003, when federal legislation was passed with the aim of revitalizing private plans through higher federal payments to the plans and creating new plan options. Medicare Advantage options include preferred provider organizations, health-maintenance organizations, and private fee-for-service and specialty plans. When you join an Advantage plan, Medicare provides a fixed payment to the plan to cover your Part A (hospital) and Part B (medical insurance) coverage. There are usually additional copayments and deductibles, depending on the type of plan you join. The plans are offered at the state level, so you need to compare what's available in your area.

Advantage plans are required to use any savings they achieve between the government payments they receive and their costs to either reduce premiums or improve the benefits they offer. The plans also can offer—and charge for—supplemental benefits such as vision, hearing, and dental care.

Many Advantage plans also include prescription-drug coverage. Another option is a new type of private Medicare plan—Part D—which has been available since 2006.

Medicare D plans are suitable for people who want to stick with traditional Medicare and their current health-care providers but would like to add a prescription-drug benefit.

Enrolling for Medicare

Although Medicare eligibility starts at age 65, enrollment isn't automatic unless you've already begun receiving Social Security benefits. In that case, your Medicare card will be mailed to you three months before your eligibility date.

Here are the enrollment options for basic Medicare, Medigap, and supplemental plans:

➤ **Enroll for Social Security and Medicare simultaneously at age 65.** Visit your local Social Security office or call the Social Security Administration at 1-800-772-1213. You can apply online in most cases (http://socialsecurity.gov). To ensure that your Medicare Part B coverage start date is not delayed, you should apply three months before the month you turn 65.

➤ **Apply for Medicare only.** Even if you plan to delay receiving Social Security benefits, you can apply for Medicare through the Social Security Administration, using any of the options listed above.

➤ **Medigap.** Many Medicare beneficiaries opt to purchase an optional Medigap policy, which charges an extra premium but caps your out-of-pocket costs. If you plan to buy a Medigap policy, do so during the six-month open-enrollment period, which is open for six months at the time you turn 65 or enroll in Medicare Part B. After the open enrollment, you may be required to take medical screening tests and can be rejected because of preexisting conditions.

➤ **Medicare Advantage.** Join these managed-care and pre-scription drug plans when you first become eligible for basic Medicare or during the annual enrollment window (November 15 to December 31). You can also enroll from January 1 to March 31 each year but can't join or switch to a plan with prescription-drug coverage during this period unless you already have drug coverage elsewhere.

➤ **Medicare D prescription-drug coverage.** The simplest option is to sign up when you first become eligible for Medicare (three months before the month you turn age 65 until three months after you turn age 65). If you don't enroll and you change your mind later, you can add prescription-drug coverage during the annual November 15–December 31 enrollment window. Unfortunately, shopping for these plans is an annual chore; plan providers usually make changes in the drugs covered and other features of the plan every year—and your drug needs may change from year to year. As a result, your costs can vary by $1,000 or more depending on the plan you choose.

➤ **Extra help.** Low-income seniors can qualify for subsidies on Part D plans which, in many cases, cover all prescription drug costs. The "Extra Help" program, administered by the Social Security Administration, is offered to seniors with income up to $16,245 a year for singles and $21,855 for married couples living together. The value of stocks, bonds, and bank accounts can't exceed $12,510 for singles and $25,010 for married couples; the income definition doesn't include the value of homes, automobiles, life insurance policies, or outside assistance from friends or relatives.

The Medicare Web site has an excellent tool that can be used to compare and shop for Advantage and Medicare D plans. Another great resource is your local State Health Insurance Assistance Program (SHIP), a government-sponsored free counseling service for Medicare beneficiaries (www.hapnetwork.org/ship-locator/).

Finally, you have the option to go with a Medigap policy. With these supplemental plans, you pay premiums in return for a policy that caps your out-of-pocket costs. You can choose among a variety of plan options that feature escalating premiums and levels of protection.

How Will Medicare Change in the Years Ahead?

Opponents of health-care reform issued dire warnings that the new law would mean death panels, slashed Medicare benefits, and totalitarian takeovers of hospitals and doctors' offices.

But the new law doesn't cut traditional Medicare benefits. Rather, it contains some important improvements to traditional Medicare aimed at boosting preventive care. For instance, starting in 201_, Medicare patients will be able to get an annual wellness visit—with no co-payment or deductible. And over time, the reform law closes the Med_care D prescription drug coverage gap—the famed doughnut hole. Currently, coverage is cut off when a beneficiary's annual out-of-pocket spending hits $2,830, and resumes at the catastrophic level ($4,550 out of pocket).

The law does reduce reimbursements to Medicare Advantage plans over a period of years to bring the program in line with traditional Medicare—although that won't necessarily translate into sharp cuts in benefits to patients.

Health-Care Shocks: The Preretirement Years

Medicare may seem complicated, but it's a health-insurance paradise compared with the problems facing retirees under age 65.

I hear often from readers of my newspaper column in their fifties and early sixties who are experiencing the disaster of job loss and de facto early retirement. Their stress and anxiety is palpable, and health insurance is one of their biggest worries. Coverage from former employers is set to expire or already is gone. Medicare benefits may be years away, and preexisting medical conditions often make it impossible to purchase a good policy in the individual insurance market.

However, health reform will improve the choices for the pre-Medicare crowd. Here's a look at the current options, and what will be changing.

COBRA

The acronym is short for the Consolidated Omnibus Budget Reconciliation Act of 1985—a law that required most employers with group health plans to let employees continue their participation in the plans if they were laid off, terminated, or experienced some other change in employment status. As a COBRA participant, you pay 100 percent of the plan's premium plus administrative fees, but you do get the benefit of your employer's group insurance rates and benefits. Coverage typically is available for 18 months after termination.

COBRA premiums are too expensive for most individuals and families, but this has been an important option in the pre-reform era for people who can't get an individual policy. Also, the Economic Recovery and Reinvestment Act of 2009 provided help for some laid-off workers by paying 65 percent of the cost of their COBRA premiums. Initially, the benefit was available only to workers laid off in the fall of 2008 or during 2009 and offered nine months of coverage. But the subsidy was extended in late 2009.

There is another possible route to COBRA subsidies. If you lost your job because of trade policies such as competition from exports or overseas outsourcing, then you can get help paying as much as 80 percent of COBRA premiums through the Trade Adjustment Assistance Reform Act of 2002. Under this law, you can receive monthly payments or a year-end tax credit to offset COBRA premiums for up to three years.

If none of these options work, you'll need to shop for an individual policy. In the pre-reform era, these policies were expensive and difficult to obtain, especially for older Americans. But the individual insurance market will change under health reform.

Starting in 2014, insurance companies won't be able to refuse applicants with pre-existing conditions. Starting immediately, insurers can't rescind coverage if you get ill, and they can't cap the lifetime dollar value of your coverage. The new law also creates new insurance options for people who need individual coverage. Starting mid-year in 2010, new, temporary high-risk insurance pools will launch for those who have been without coverage for six months and have pre-existing conditions. These pools are intended to serve as a bridge to longer-term solutions. State-based insurance exchanges will operate starting in 2014, and Medicaid will be expanded to more low-income households over the next few years. Coverage will be made available to all individuals under age 65 with incomes up to 133 percent of the federal poverty level—in 2010, $22,050 for a family of four.

Most people will have to buy health insurance starting in 2014, but tax credits will be available on a sliding income-based scale to help make the coverage affordable. Although insurance companies won't be allowed to consider pre-existing conditions when pricing policies, they will be permitted to vary their rates somewhat based on age.

It's important to look closely at the specifics of any insurance plan you consider buying. Contact your state insurance departments for details and guidance. Also see **Figure 7.2** for more insurance shopping tips.

Figure 7.2 Questions to Ask When Evaluating Individual Health-Insurance Policies

> ➤ What will I actually be charged in premiums given my age and health risks?
>
> ➤ How big is the deductible?
>
> ➤ What are the copayments and other out-of-pocket costs?
>
> ➤ What benefits are covered? If I face an unexpected serious illness such as cancer, will this policy adequately protect me?
>
> ➤ What prescription drugs are covered? Is there a formulary (list of drugs that are covered)?
>
> ➤ Will I have to change health-care providers? Do I have to use doctors and hospitals in the plan's network? Will I be charged a higher rate if I go out of network?
>
> ➤ Is the plan reputable? Check with your state department of insurance to make sure the plan is licensed and to find out if any complaints have been filed against it and whatever details are available.
>
> ➤ What is the quality of care provided by this plan? Are there public data about member satisfaction or about, for example, how well doctors in the plan follow up with patients who have been sick? Some state insurance departments provide comparative quality information. The National Committee for Quality Assurance also posts public report cards about plans that it accredits (online at www.ncqa.org).

Source: Families USA.

Long-Term Care

Let's say you've done a good job saving for retirement—and even have your basic health-care costs covered. Just one more question: Have you planned for the possibility that you might need long-term care?

About two-thirds of people over 65 will need some form of long-term care during their lives, and they will need help for an average of three years.[4] Medicare's coverage of long-term care is very limited. The program pays for some home health care, skilled nursing, and hospice care, but it won't cover most nursing-home care or at-home services such as a home care aide.

There really are only a few ways to meet this kind of need. A family member can provide care—and that's the most common solution. But can you count on a family member to meet a need that could be many years down the road?

You could self-fund your care if you're sufficiently wealthy—but do you want to burn through substantial portion of your retirement assets to pay for long-term care when that money could be earning a return and funding retirement for your spouse if you're no longer around?

The cost of care can be crippling. Nursing home care costs around $70,000 per year, assisted living facilities run around $36,000 per year, and home health care costs an average of $29 per hour.[5]

Medicaid is an option for some people. The federal program that provides health insurance to the poor actually is the largest funder of long-term care, paying for about 40 percent of all care delivered in the United States. But Medicaid pays for long-term care only if you are indigent or receive Social Security disability payments. Some people begin by paying for care out of pocket and go on Medicaid later after their resources have been exhausted. There are other drawbacks. For example, you may not be able to meet Medicaid's test for significant medical need. Also, the facility of your choice may not accept Medicaid, and you might need to go to a location far from family and friends.

Medicaid is administered at the state level, and income eligibility rules vary by state. Generally, however, an individual can't have more than $2,000 in assets ($3,000 for couples).

The other option is to purchase a long-term care insurance policy. Long-term care insurance generally covers a range of health-care and personal needs outside of what Medicare or health insurance would fund. Although these policies have been around for about 30 years, they've been slow to catch on—just 9 percent of Americans age 55 and older have bought long-term care insurance, according to The Urban Institute.

The policies got off to a rocky start. In the early days, some underwriters priced policies too aggressively and then boosted premiums sharply for existing customers. More recently, the market has settled down to a handful of solid, established insurance companies. And tougher regulation by state insurance boards has eliminated most questionable rate-hike practices.

It's not an appropriate financial product if you have low income and qualify for Medicaid. It's also not for you unless you're confident that you can keep paying the premiums over what could be a very long time—if not, you could wind up throwing money down the drain by buying insurance and then letting your coverage lapse.

Expense is the main hurdle for consumers; a recent study by Fidelity Investments estimated lifetime premium costs for an average 65-year-old couple at $85,000.

If you do decide to buy a policy, it's important to shop carefully and get good advice. Long-term care policies are complex. Insurance companies can't cancel long-term care policies and can't change the terms—but neither can you. Here are some of the key decisions you'll need to make.

Daily benefit. Most experts recommend policies that cover $150 in daily expenses. Be sure to get a policy with a provision that adjusts the daily bene-fit annually for inflation and allows for care to be provided in your home.

Length of coverage. A policy that covers benefits for a two-year period is adequate in most cases, and situations requiring more than four years are rare.

Elimination period. Similar to a deductible, the elimination period is the length of time you pay for care before benefits kick in. The period on most policies ranges from 20 to 120 days; if you're able to finance your initial care for a few months, then a longer elimination period will get you a significantly lower premium.

Shared coverage. If you're married, consider getting a shared policy that features a discounted premium and flexible access to benefits for you and your spouse. Let's say you buy a policy offering two years of benefits for each partner, and the husband subsequently goes into a nursing home and exhausts his benefits. The couple has the option of tapping into the spouse's benefits to continue paying the husband's expenses.

Also, look into whether you can buy long-term care insurance at work. Your employer can't subsidize the cost, but you'll probably benefit from attractive group rates and confidence that a quality underwriter has been selected. This approach has been gaining in popularity, and more than 40 percent of employers now offer policies to employees or their spouses, according to Hewitt Associates, the employee-benefits consulting firm.

If you purchase an individual policy, stick with one of the major carriers with solid financial ratings—and one that has never raised premiums on its existing customers. Financial planners can help you select an underwriter and sort through the thicket of feature choices; you can also find a broker on your own through the American Association for Long-Term Care Insurance.

The new health-care reform law establishes a new long-term care option that was championed by the late Senator Edward M. Kennedy—a government-sponsored voluntary national insurance trust similar to Social Security called the Community Living Assistance Services and Supports (CLASS) Act.

CLASS launches in 2011, and it will be financed through voluntary payroll deductions. All working adults will be enrolled automatically unless they choose to opt out. After a five-year vesting period, any plan participant (regardless of age) needing care will be eligible to receive a daily benefit—probably $50 to $75—to offset the cost of in-home or nursing facility care.

Resources

Medicare

Medicare and You handbook. The U.S. Department of Health and Human Services publishes an annual guide explaining everything you'd ever want to know about Medicare. A copy is mailed every fall to current recipients, but it also can be downloaded free as a PDF (www.medicare.gov/Publications/Pubs/pdf/10050.pdf).

Comparing Medicare options. The Medicare Web site offers an online tool that lets you compare traditional Medicare with Advantage, Medigap, and Part D plans (www.medicare.gov/MPPF).

Track your benefits. Current beneficiaries can view claim status, order forms and cards, and view eligibility information (http://mymedicare.gov/).

Extra help. Low-income seniors can learn how to apply for a subsidy of prescription drug costs at https://secure.ssa.gov/apps6z/i1020/main.html.

National Medicare hotline. Medicare will answer questions about the basic program, prescription-drug benefits, and Medicare Advantage plans at its national hotline (1-800-MEDICARE).

Online guide. The Henry J. Kaiser Family Foundation's Web site maintains a well-respected online guide to Medicare (www.kff.org/medicare/7067/ataglance.cfm).

Medicare Part D shopping. Use the Medicare Web site's Prescription Drug Plan Finder (http://tinyurl.com/yh7x6vm) during the annual November 15–December 31 enrollment window to get a detailed analysis of plans, estimated annual costs, monthly premiums, annual deductibles, gap coverage, drug coverage, and customer satisfaction ratings. You'll plug in a list of your prescriptions by name, dosage, and number of pills taken monthly. The finder also offers important details on drug utilization and restrictions.

Medicare Advantage shopping. Use the Medicare Options Compare tool (http://tinyurl.com/y9dqal) to compare Advantage HMO and PPO plans. You'll find information on premiums, drug coverage, provider choices, and customer satisfaction ratings. The tool will also let you compare these managed-care offerings with traditional Medicare coverage.

Health-care provider quality. The U.S. Department of Health and Human Services Web site offers a database showing how well hospitals care for patients with various medical conditions or who have undergone specific surgical procedures (http://hospitalcompare.hhs.gov).

State-by-state online resources. The Kaiser Foundation's directory to state-level Web sites and agencies can also provide assistance (www.kff.org/medicare/7067/med_resources.cfm#resources).

Fee-based advice. If you're willing to pay a bit for some additional hand-holding and services, use one of the fee-based counseling services that have sprung up. For a price ranging from $200 to $300, Allsup Medicare Advisor® (www.allsup.com/) provides a detailed analysis of your health status and plan needs; the company also double-checks the information in the Medicare database with insurance plans and health providers.

COBRA

FAQs on retirement and health benefits for dislocated workers.
The U.S. Department of Labor's Employee Benefits Security Administration maintains a Web page that offers details on your rights under federal law to various health coverage extensions (www.dol.gov/ebsa/publications/dislocated_workers_brochure.html).

Hotline. The U.S. Department of Labor also maintains a free counseling hotline to answer your questions (1-866-444-3272).

Backgrounder. Families USA, a not-for-profit health-care advocacy group, also has posted a page with detailed information about the federal COBRA subsidy (www.familiesusa.org/issues/private-insurance/understanding-cobra-premium.html).

Veterans. Veterans can access a wide range of health-care services through the Department of Veterans Affairs. More information is available at the VA Web site (www1.va.gov/health/index.asp) or toll free phone line (1-877-227-8387).

Chapter Notes

1. Federal Interagency Forum on Aging-Related Statistics, *Older Americans 2008: Key Indicators of Well-Being* (www.agingstats.gov/agingstatsdotnet/main_site/default.aspx).
2. M. G. Gluck and V. Reno (Eds.), *Reflections on Implementing Medicare* (Washington, DC: National Academy of Social Insurance, January 2001).
3. Henry J. Kaiser Family Foundation, *Medicare: A Primer* (www.kff.org/medicare/7615.cfm).
4. Howard Gleckman, *The Role of Private Insurance in Financing Long-Term Care* (Chestnut Hill, MA: Center for Retirement Research at Boston College, September 2007).
5. Henry J. Kaiser Family Foundation, Medicaid and Long-Term Care Services and Supports (February 2009) (www.kff.org/medicaid/2186.cfm).

CHAPTER 8

Taxes and Retirement

BENJAMIN FRANKLIN FAMOUSLY SAID, "In this world, nothing can be said to be certain, except death and taxes."

Retirement is less certain these days—but if you do retire, expect to pay taxes. Your income may well be lower, which will lighten your income-tax burden, but a number of new factors come into play that affect your tax situation. These will concern your retirement savings, Social Security, and any continued income from work. In this chapter, we'll look at some of the key tax issues and decisions you'll face in retirement.

Walking Out the Door: Pension Decisions

When you retire, you'll need to make some decisions about your accumulated benefits, including any 401(k) or traditional defined benefit pensions. Enrollees in 401(k) plans always have the option to take a lump sum—and so can many traditional pension recipients. You may be tempted to do just that—although it's almost always better not to do so. Pension recipients usually do better opting for a lifetime-annuity payment option. If you have a 401(k), it makes sense to delay paying taxes on those assets as long as possible.

Traditional pension. If your employer provides a defined benefit pension, then you'll pay personal income tax on distributions you receive from the plan. That's because private pensions receive favorable tax treatment at every other step along the way. Employers get to deduct their contributions. Investment earnings on plan assets aren't taxed, and employees aren't taxed on contributions at the time they are made. If you decide at retirement to accept your pension as a lump sum, then the income-tax bill can be sizable. Taxes aside, there are other reasons for most retirees to opt for a lifetime of annuity-style payments rather than a lump sum (see Chapter 4).

401(k). Your choices with a 401(k) include taking a lump sum, making a direct rollover to an IRA, or simply leaving 401(k) assets in your employer's plan. Taking a lump sum can generate a significant tax bill, especially if your account—plus your final year of wages—totals enough to put you in a high tax bracket. If you do decide to roll over your account to an IRA, then make sure the check is made out to your new custodian; otherwise, your employer must withhold 20 percent of your funds for taxes even if you plan to roll the money over. And if you don't complete your rollover within 60 days, all the money is subject to income tax plus a 10 percent penalty if you're younger than 59½.

Required Minimum Distributions

The tax-deferred party must end sometime, and if you're older than 70½, you'll have to take an annual required minimum distribution (RMD) from your traditional IRA or 401(k) funds and report it as income. (Technically, you must take your first RMD by April 1 of the year after the year you turn 70½.) Your RMD is determined using an IRS formula that divides your account balance by life expectancy calculated using an actuarial projection. You can determine the minimum to withdraw using an online calculator or by downloading IRS Publication 590, which contains the tables. If you fail to take your RMD, then you'll pay a stiff penalty—50 percent of the amount you failed to withdraw. Talk with your retirement-account custodian or accountant about the various options available to make sure you comply—but remember that the responsibility to take an RMD ultimately is yours.

Multiple accounts. The law doesn't require that you take an RMD for each IRA you own. If you have more than one IRA, you can simply add them all together, calculate your RMD, and make the withdrawal from a single account. The benefit here: You can pick whatever account does the least damage to your holdings. If one account has taken losses and you'd prefer to give it time to recover, make your RMD from a different account.

RMDs were suspended for 2009 as part of an economic relief measure for investors hit hard by the market crash; the RMD for that year would have been a double whammy because the distributions would be calculated against account balances that were higher in 2008 and funded by the sale of assets that had since fallen substantially. Of course, the relief measure only helped people who didn't need the minimums to fund living expenses. Relief measures aside, you're generally better off spending money outside tax-sheltered accounts before tapping into those accounts. "You want to put off paying the income taxes as long as possible," says IRA plan distribution expert Jim Lange. "If you spend the IRA dollars first, that accelerates your tax payments. When you do that, you will always run out of money faster than the person who spends the after-tax money first because you've taken funds out of a tax-sheltered account and those funds are no longer there to keep growing."

The other downside of RMDs is the hit you take to fund income taxes. "Say you want to spend $50,000," says Lange. "If you take it out of your IRA, that triggers a tax of about $13,000. After you pay the tax, you only have $37,000 and you have to go into other funds for the rest of what you need."

Roth IRAs

There is one way to avoid or minimize your RMDs—with a Roth IRA.

Roths were introduced in the late 1990s, and they've been gaining popularity steadily in recent years. With a Roth, you can invest after-tax income up to a specified amount each year; earnings on the account are tax free, and tax-free withdrawals can be made after age 59½ But Roths are still somewhat underappreciated, especially among older retirement savers who became investors before Roths came on the scene. In 2008, only 15.9 percent of American households owned a Roth IRA.[1]

You can't contribute pretax dollars to a Roth, and while that might sound like a disadvantage, Roths have some features that are very positive for older investors.

➤ RMDs: Unlike traditional IRAs, you aren't required to take annual distributions from a Roth when you turn 70½. That makes Roths a good vehicle for intergenerational wealth transfer, as you can hang on to the money and bequeath the holdings to your heirs tax free. But your heirs generally will have to take minimum payouts from the inherited Roth over their lifetimes.

➤ With a Roth IRA, you've paid the income tax up front because you invested post-tax dollars. That means your withdrawals aren't subject to income (or capital gains) taxes so long as the account has been open five years and you are at least 59½ years old. Your Roth IRA can continue to grow tax free for as long as you own it.

➤ Beginning in 2010, a change in federal law has removed the household income limit for eligibility to convert traditional IRAs to Roth accounts. Previously, only households with modified adjusted gross income of less than $100,000 were eligible to make Roth conversions.

➤ Roths also can be a good tax hedge if you believe—as I do—that today's historically low federal income-tax rates are destined to rise in the years ahead. Why? The federal government is awash in trillions of dollars of debt; Medicare and Social Security programs both face major fiscal problems that will have to be fixed, and they are projected to consume about three-quarters of all federal spending by the middle of this century. It stands to reason that higher taxes will be needed to offset those bills; if you think taxes will be higher when you retire than they are today, then you can use a Roth to take advantage of today's income-tax rates.

Older investors should give serious consideration to converting some portion of tax sheltered investments to a Roth—with these caveats:

➤ **Immediate tax liability.** A Roth conversion isn't right for every investor because you need to be able to fund the tax liability generated by moving your funds out of a tax-sheltered account. Consider this carefully before doing a conversion and only convert the portion that you're sure you can fund. If your retirement portfolio is depressed, it's a good time to move dollars out of traditional tax-sheltered IRAs to taxable Roth IRAs; the value of the funds you move is taxable now—which means you can more easily move a greater amount of equity holdings.

➤ **Future tax policy.** When you convert to a Roth, you're making a bet of sorts on future federal tax policy that might or might not work in your favor. Some financial planners are cautioning investors not to put too big a bet on Roths given the ballooning federal deficit and looming pressure on spending from rising federal expenses for programs such as Medicare, Social Security, and health-care reform. Some people worry that Washington might try to raise revenue by pulling the rug out from Roths' tax-free status or subjecting them to capital gains taxes.

At the end of the day, it's impossible to make investing decisions today on changes in policy that might occur. So don't put all your eggs in one basket. It's best to employ a balanced mix of tax-deferred and taxable retirement accounts. Against that background, Roths can play an invaluable role.

Social Security and Medicare Taxes

Americans pay federal income taxes on Social Security benefits in situations where overall annual income exceeds certain levels. No one is taxed on more than 85 percent of their benefits, and the level of income tax paid is determined by your *combined income*. The federal government defines combined income as follows:[2]

Adjusted gross income
+ Nontaxable interest
+ ½ of Social Security benefits
_____

= Combined income

Filing an individual return. If you file a federal tax return as an individual and your combined income is between $25,000 and $34,000, then you may be taxed on as much as 50 percent of your benefits. If your combined income is higher than $34,000, as much as 85 percent of your benefits may be taxable.

Filing a joint return. If you and your spouse have combined income between $32,000 and $44,000, then you may pay income taxes on as much as 50 percent of your benefits. If your combined income is more than $44,000, as much as 85 percent of benefits may be taxable.

After you begin receiving Social Security benefits, you'll get a benefit statement in the mail every January (Form SSA-1099) that shows the amount of benefits you received in the previous year; use that statement when you do your tax return to determine if your benefits will be subject to tax in that year.

Medicare. If you continue to work in retirement—even after filing to receive Social Security—you'll continue to pay Medicare FICA taxes on any earned income that you generate.

Resources
Roth IRAs

Fairmark Press. Tax adviser Kaye Thomas runs Fairmark Press and publishes *Guide to Roth IRA, 401k and 403b Retirement Accounts*, a useful online guide to retirement-account tax matters (http://fairmark .com/rothira/index.htm).

IRS. The online *IRA Online Resource Guide—Information About Roth IRAs* offers information about tax treatment of Roth accounts (www.irs.gov/retirement/article/0,,id=137307,00.html).

Required Minimum Distributions

IRS. A page of frequently asked questions on required distributions can be found at www.irs.gov/retirement/article/0,,id=96989,00.html#4.

IRS Form 590. Information on Publication 590, Individual Retirement Arrangements, can be found at www.irs.gov/publications/p590/index.html.

AARP. AARP has an online calculator that will help you figure out your RMD (www.aarp.org/money/toolkit/articles/required_minimum _distribution_calculator.html).

Social Security and Taxes

IRS. One page at www.irs.gov/taxtopics/tc423.html describes the taxation of Social Security benefits.

Social Security Administration. Situations in which Social Security benefits are taxed are described online at www.ssa.gov/planners/taxes.htm.

Chapter Notes

1. Investment Company Institute, *2009 Investment Company Fact Book*, 49th ed., p. 89 (http://icifactbook.org), accessed August 2009.
2. Social Security Administration, "Taxes and Your Social Security Benefits" (www.ssa.gov/planners/taxes.htm), accessed August 2009.

CHAPTER 9

Coping with Post-Bubble Real Estate

WHEN THE HOUSING MARKET was soaring, many baby boomers thought of their homes as piggy banks that could be cracked open to fund retirement. High housing prices would allow them to leverage their equity to finance lifestyles, buy second homes, or pay entry fees into retirement communities. That thinking was encouraged by lenders, who aggressively marketed low-interest mortgage debt and equity-to-cash products such as home-equity loans and reverse mortgages.

Now the housing bubble has burst. High unemployment rates, sagging incomes, and rising foreclosure rates mean we're not likely to see a strong rebound anytime soon in the housing market. But planning for your retirement housing needs raises other questions unrelated to the current market. Is a move really the right decision for you, or can your current residence be adapted to serve your needs? What role can technology play in your future retirement residence? Most important, can you shed the costly burden of a mortgage ahead of retirement?

In this chapter, we'll look at what you can expect from the changing real estate market and consider some practical ways to respond.

The Real Estate Wake-Up Call

Older Americans have more exposure to real estate than any other demographic group. Seventy-nine percent of Americans age 55 and older own their own homes, compared with a national median ownership rate of 69 percent.[1] As the bubble inflated, older homeowners took on larger mortgages, and a greater percentage are carrying mortgage debt well into their sixties than ever before.[2]

For the boomer generation now approaching retirement, home equity accounts for one-third to one-half of all net worth. The only larger source of household wealth is Social Security. The housing crash affects a much larger group of Americans than does a volatile stock market, simply because home ownership is spread much more evenly across income groups (see **Figure 9.1**).[3]

Older Americans are just beginning to come to terms with a housing market that has changed for the foreseeable future. In some metropolitan areas, prices are down more than 30 percent from their peak, and a record 19 million homes in the United States stand vacant.[4] The effect on boomers has been dramatic; one study suggests that 30 percent of Americans ages 45 to 54 are "underwater" on their mortgages—that is, they owe more than their homes are worth and would need to bring cash to a closing.[5]

Warning signs about housing were flashing well ahead of the crash. Baby boomers drove housing demand over the past several decades as they reached adulthood and started families. Now boomers are becoming an enormous group of potential home sellers as we make plans to downsize or move. But the pool of younger potential buyers is smaller and less affluent. "The most important factor that pushes

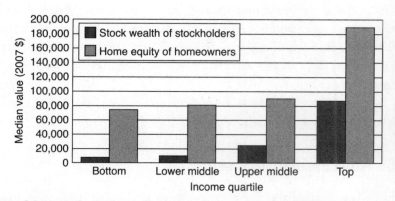

Figure 9.1 Home Equity Versus Stocks as a Source of Household Wealth

Note: Income quartiles are equal fourths of all households sorted by pretax income.

Source: The State of the Nation's Housing 2009, Joint Center for Housing Studies, Harvard University; reprinted with permission.

Going Mortgage-Free

Older Americans are carrying more mortgage debt in retirement than at any time in the past. But if you have the cash, consider bucking the trend by paying off your mortgage before you retire. This can be a good way to reduce your recurring expenses in retirement. In addition, the interest expense on your mortgage almost certainly is greater than the returns you'd earn on age-appropriate fixed-income investments such as certificates of deposit, Treasury bills, or Treasury bonds.*

If you do have cash on hand available to pay down a mortgage, use lower-return taxable savings before tapping tax-advantaged IRAs or 401(k) accounts. But even funds from tax-advantaged accounts can make sense, argues Anthony Webb, a research economist at the Center for Retirement Research at Boston College who has studied mortgages in retirement: "If you assume a constant marginal tax rate, then even at a 28 percent rate, and even for itemizers, it's unlikely that risk-free assets, even invested in an IRA/401(k), will earn sufficient to cover the mortgage interest cost."

One caveat: Pay careful attention to your overall liquidity in shifting funds from savings accounts to mortgage payments. Make sure you retain enough liquid assets to cover your anticipated expenses and emergencies.

Note

* Anthony Webb, *Should You Carry a Mortgage into Retirement?* (Chestnut Hill, MA: Center for Retirement Research at Boston College, July 2009 (http://crr.bc.edu/briefs/should_you_carry_a_mortgage_into_retirement_.html), accessed August 2009

prices up is when you have more buyers than sellers," says Dowell Myers, a professor of urban planning and demography at the University of Southern California. Myers has been pointing to a huge sea change in the ratio of buyers and sellers that will put downward pressure on housing values over the next two decades.[6] "The baby boom generation has pushed up housing prices over the past three decades, as

[it] steadily moved up the ladder and bought housing. So people think the last three decades are normal. At some point boomers will start to cash out."

Myers thinks the future buy-sell ratios could be improved (from a seller perspective) if the rate of immigration to the United States were to increase significantly and create greater demand for housing. Likewise, so-called echo boomers—the children of baby boomers— could boost the market as they come into their prime home-buying years—*if* housing becomes sufficiently affordable and their incomes are high enough. Although prices have been plunging,[7] the affordability gap remains sizable because median incomes of first-time home buyers have been in a long-term, secular fall, dropping 15 percent since 1976. Before the crash, buying power was propped up by liberal bank-lending policies that have now been curbed.[8] That means echo boomers and immigrants aren't likely to ride to the rescue of housing without general economic improvement—and even then prices won't recover to precrash levels anytime soon.

Aging in Place

If there's any good news about housing, it's this: Most people would prefer not to sell and move during their retirement years. One AARP survey found that 89 percent of Americans want to stay in their current homes as long as possible—and that number rises to 95 percent for people 75 and older. Despite all the hype and marketing around the concept of active adult and age-restricted communities, only 3 percent of 55-plus households were living in these communities as of 2007.[9]

The housing crash will solidify the urge to stay put, but doing so successfully requires some careful planning—something few boomers are doing. (See **Figure 9.2** for a checklist of issues.) The simple truth is that few of us are thinking proactively about what it means to age in place; just 16 percent of respondents to that AARP survey said they had made modifications to their homes that would make it possible to stay where they are.

Too many of us are living in what some experts have dubbed "Peter Pan housing"—homes designed for people who plan never to get old. Pioneering approaches are emerging that will help people stay where they are and thus avoid costly and difficult relocations.

Figure 9.2 Retirement Housing Planning Checklist

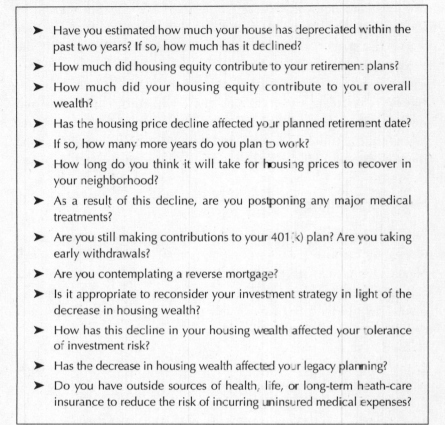

> ➤ Have you estimated how much your house has depreciated within the past two years? If so, how much has it declined?
>
> ➤ How much did housing equity contribute to your retirement plans?
>
> ➤ How much did your housing equity contribute to your overall wealth?
>
> ➤ Has the housing price decline affected your planned retirement date?
>
> ➤ If so, how many more years do you plan to work?
>
> ➤ How long do you think it will take for housing prices to recover in your neighborhood?
>
> ➤ As a result of this decline, are you postponing any major medical treatments?
>
> ➤ Are you still making contributions to your 401(k) plan? Are you taking early withdrawals?
>
> ➤ Are you contemplating a reverse mortgage?
>
> ➤ Is it appropriate to reconsider your investment strategy in light of the decrease in housing wealth?
>
> ➤ How has this decline in your housing wealth affected your tolerance of investment risk?
>
> ➤ Has the decrease in housing wealth affected your legacy planning?
>
> ➤ Do you have outside sources of health, life, or long-term health-care insurance to reduce the risk of incurring uninsured medical expenses?

Source: Adapted from Principal Financial Group report "How Housing Wealth Affects Retirement Planning"; reprinted with permission.

Universal Design

Much of the emerging thinking on aging in place concerns universal design—a set of architecture and design principles that seek to provide suitable living environments for a diverse range of people. For people who are aging, the relevant universal design ideas include adjusted heights of countertops and electrical sockets; usability of faucets, door levers, switches, and appliances; wide no-elevation entrances; comfortable height toilets; and improved lighting.

Universal design can be used in remodeling or in new home construction. Jan Cullinane, an author and retirement expert, put universal-design principles to work when she and her husband built a new home a couple of years ago in northern Florida. She started by seeking out a builder to install features such as nonskid tiles, curbless showers, levered doorknobs, and even an elevator that connects the three floors of the house. "Universal design isn't really for old people—it's really an idea that works for all people," she says.

For remodeling projects, look for contractors, architects, and designers who are certified aging-in-place specialists (CAPS) after taking special training. You can find state-by-state listings of CAPS at the Web sites of AARP and the National Association of Homebuilders.

High-Tech Aging

Baby boomers will embrace new technology that helps them age in place—no surprise given our lifelong love affair with computers, cell phones, PDAs, and other gadgets. Products already are available that can help boomers care for their own aging parents, such as home-monitoring devices. But we're likely to see much more sophisticated technologies that promote independence.

Motion sensors will interact with security systems and alert care-givers when activity isn't detected according to schedule. Automated phone systems will remind people to take their medications—and family members or caregivers will be able to help seniors manage their care long distance over video-enabled Web connections.[10] One of the world's largest technology companies—Intel Corporation—has a major initiative devoted to the development of technologies that will do everything from capturing your vital signs at home to enabling online chat with a medical professional. "We're going to have a very large group of retirees who are much more familiar with computers and cell phones. It's going to be a much more tech-savvy population," says Eric Dishman, Intel fellow and director of health innovation and policy at Intel's Digital Health Group.

Here are examples of products Intel is developing.

Preventing falls. Injuries from falls are a leading cause of hospitalization for older people and often start downward health spirals that lead to death. Intel's research suggests that perhaps half of all falls can be prevented by monitoring subtle changes in body movement. The company has developed a wearable-sensor prototype that measures the length of a person's stride and detects neurological problems or muscle mass decline. When these conditions are detected, preventative measures can be taken.

Fighting isolation. Losing the ability to drive is a major cause of isolation for older people. At a research lab in Ireland, Intel put basic GPS systems into the cars of older people who still do drive and linked them to online Google maps that display their routes to nondrivers who might need rides. "It became a ride-sharing board, using a bit of intelligent technology," Dishman says. "That is disruptive technology because it provides social contact and a way to be mobile."

Communications help for Alzheimer's patients. Intel has been working on what Dishman calls "caller I.D. on steroids. It's a small screen that sits next to a patient's landline phone and displays a photo of the caller, along with a short text blurb describing who the person is, the last time you spoke, and what you discussed. The blurb is there because the patient typed a few notes into a database after that last conversation."

Age-Friendly Communities: The Beacon Hill Village Model

Aging in place also depends on strong community support. "Housing isn't just about geographic location," says Elinor Ginzler, director of livable communities for AARP. "It's about the bigger picture of the design of the house and community—how it keeps you engaged." Ginzler oversees AARP's work encouraging communities to develop age-friendly policies, and she doesn't think many are ready for aging populations. Consider whether your community offers key aging-in-place amenities such as good public transportation, one-stop shopping locations, shuttle services, and age-appropriate fitness and community centers. Will you have access to friends and family as well as ways to stay engaged?

"Gerontologists define aging successfully as feeling optimistic and in charge and financially in a position to live out the rest of your life the way you want to," Ginzler says. "You want to feel a sense of control over yourself and the world around you."

In some parts of the country, residents have banded together to form associations that can provide necessary services. The leading model is the so-called intentional community, a not-for-profit, consumer-led approach to supporting aging in place. The pioneer in this movement is Beacon Hill Village (BHV), which was launched in 2002 and serves central Boston. It's a grassroots community founded by a small group of residents who wanted to stay in their homes as they grew old rather than move to a senior community. It's a virtual community that brings services to people where they live rather than moving people to services in institutional settings. The youngest members are in their early fifties, and the oldest is over 100; their health ranges from very good to people who have serious needs.

BHV offers its members three key services: a concierge, living assistance, and community.

➤ **Concierge.** BHV maintains a database of vetted service providers and can refer them to members—and serves as a go-between if the need arises to advocate on members' behalf. Service providers include everything from personal trainers to dog walkers, health clubs, and geriatric-care management.

➤ **Living assistance.** BHV can arrange all kinds of in-home services such as meal delivery, transportation, social services, and even hospice care.

➤ **Community.** This component is especially important for people living alone. BHV offers seminars, trips, lectures, exercise classes, and wellness and prevention programs. "It's as though you lived in a high-level continuing-care retirement community, but the people who started it and choose to be part of it are passionate about being in their own homes for the rest of their lives," says Judy Willett, BHV's executive director.

Although Beacon Hill started as a grassroots community effort, today it has a professional staff and is funded through annual membership fees ($600 for an individual and $890 for a household) plus additional charges for discounted à la carte services; subsidies are available for individuals who can't afford the full fee.

Continuing-Care Retirement Communities

The paralysis in residential real estate has made it very difficult for seniors to sell their homes when the time comes to move for health or lifestyle reasons.

One type of housing affected by the housing crash is the continuing-care retirement community (CCRC), which typically requires a large up-front payment upon entry. This allows seniors to stay in a single location that can meet their health-care needs for the remainder of their lives.

"It's usually structured so that you can take equity from the house, make that your entrance fee, and then pay monthly based on need," says Larry Minnix, chief executive officer of the American Association of Homes and Services for the Aging, an association of not-for-profit organizations that offer a continuum of aging services ranging from adult day services to CCRCs.

The slide in housing values and stock portfolios has translated into declining CCRC applications, and some communities are responding by providing assistance to would-be home sellers. "Some are suspending or postponing entry fees," Minnix says. "Others are providing bridge loans or retaining real estate specialists to help people prepare and sell their homes. Everyone is trying to get creative in providing help."

Reverse mortgages are another potential source of help. Recent changes in federal rules make it possible to use these home-equity conversion mortgages (HECMs) to purchase a new home. An HECM can't be used for moves into retirement communities where the residents don't own equity (such as CCRCs), but the new rule can help facilitate sell-and-buy transactions by giving a seller the flexibility to accept a lower price and still afford a move.

Some CCRCs also are starting to deliver services to people living in homes in their surrounding areas.

Intentional communities are growing quickly. Beacon Hill's membership has grown from 70 when the community was founded in 2002 to 450 currently, and about 75 percent of members typically renew their annual memberships. In 2008 and 2009, 48 new communities were formed around the country, and Willett says hundreds have been attending Beacon Hill's workshops, which are designed to help people start their own intentional communities.

Moving and Downsizing

If your retirement living plan calls for a move, this much is clear: There's no point waiting for things to get better. Odds are that 10 to 20 years will pass before housing prices reach precrash levels.[11] Although you may need to take a hit on your selling price, you'll also pay less for your next residence, so don't let the current market put you into a state of "analysis paralysis."

One attractive option is downsizing if you've got more space than you need—a move that can provide a nice cash windfall. If you downsize by selling your primary residence and purchasing something less expensive, federal tax law permits you to keep as much as $250,000 of the gain tax free if you're single ($500,000 for couples). That money can be used any way you like; the rule applies so long as you've lived in the home you're selling for at least two of the last five years.

Reverse Mortgages

One way to tap into your home's equity in a tough economy is to secure a reverse mortgage. If you're over age 62, you can use a reverse mortgage to convert a portion of your home equity into cash and continue living in the house. The reverse-mortgage business has been growing quickly over the last several years, despite high fees and a history of abusive sales practices by some lenders.

A reverse mortgage is an interest-bearing loan secured by the equity in your home. It can be a useful tool if you need to free up equity for a large expense or a medical need such as long-term care or if you face the threat of losing your home altogether because you can't make mortgage payments. But a reverse mortgage should be viewed as a last resort used for necessities, not for dream trips or other luxuries.

Most important, approach reverse mortgages with a great deal of caution. Make sure you understand how the loan works and what you're getting into. Steer clear of any lender selling bundles of financial products alongside the loan. One abusive practice used by some lenders involves using proceeds from a reverse mortgage to fund an annuity; generally, that's a scam because the annuity proceeds usually fall short of the loan costs.

Reverse mortgages offer a way to spend down the equity you've built in your home. But unlike a traditional mortgage or home-equity line, you don't have to make payments on the loan until the home is no longer used as a principal residence—typically when you die or move into a nursing home. At that point, the principal and interest accrued on the loan are due in full. (The amount owed can't exceed the value of your home; if your home is sold and the proceeds exceed the amount owed on the mortgage, the excess funds go to you or your estate.) Another benefit: Reverse mortgages have a "nonrecourse" feature, which means the amount owed can't exceed the appraised value of the home. If the value falls below the loan amount, then the lender is on the hook for the difference.

The most typical loan type is a home-equity conversion mortgage (HECM), which is insured by the Federal Housing Administration. Reforms contained in the Housing and Economic Recovery Act of 2008 made it easier to use HECMs by raising the loan limit to $417,000 nationally and to $625,500 in areas of the country where housing values are relatively high. The new law also capped loan-origination fees at 2 percent of the first $200,000 borrowed and 1 percent for any amount beyond that. Overall, origination fees can't exceed $6,000.

Federal law requires that borrowers receive a free counseling session with a loan counselor approved by the U.S. Department of Housing and Urban Development—usually at a not-for-profit organization or public agency. Make sure you find a counselor who is knowledgeable and independent; the Financial Industry Regulatory Authority recommends asking any counselor suggested by a lender whether he receives any funding from either the lender or the mortgage industry.[12] Even if you are applying for a loan that is not federally guaranteed, it is a good idea to get advice from a trusted financial adviser who has no interest in either the mortgage or any investment you plan to make with the proceeds.

Resources

Reverse Mortgages

Decumulation.org. The Web site of the not-for-profit National Endowment for Financial Education (NEFE) (www.decumulation.org/HomeMortgage/ReverseMortgages/tabid/73/Default.aspx) offers an explanation of reverse mortgages as well as loan scenarios. The NEFE site was developed by more than twenty financial-planning, academic, and financial services executives, regulators, and the federal government.

AARP reverse mortgage calculator. An online calculator (http://rmc.ibisreverse.com//rmc_pages/rmc_aarp/aarp_index.aspx) from AARP provides approximate estimates for several federally insured reverse mortgages. It allows you to get a ballpark estimate of how much cash you might be able to obtain through a reverse mortgage.

National Council on aging reverse mortgage initiative. "Use Your Home to Stay at Home" (www.ncoa.org/calendar-of-events/webinars/reverse-mortgage-use-your.html) is aimed at helping older Americans leverage their home equity in responsible ways in order to stay in their homes.

Universal Design

Guidelines. Toolbase, a site sponsored by the National Association of Home Builders, offers a handy and very exhaustive list of features to consider in new construction or renovation projects (http://toolbase.org/ToolbaseResources/level4DG.aspx?ContentDetailID=3638&BucketID=2&CategoryID=22).

Contractor directory. Builders, architects, and designers can now become certified aging-in-place specialists (CAPS) after taking special training. You can find state-by-state listings of CAPS at the Web sites of AARP and the National Association of Homebuilders (http://www.nahb.org/directory.aspx?sectionID=126&directoryID=188).

Intentional Communities

Beacon Hill Village. BHV (www.beaconhillvillage.org) is an acknowledged pioneer in the intentional communities movement.

Beacon Hill also sells a how-to manual (www.beaconhillvillage.org/building.html) that offers step-by-step instructions on how to form an intentional community. AARP has produced a video about Beacon Hill (http://assets.aarp.org/external_sites/caregiving/multimedia/CG_BeaconHill.html).

Village to Village Network. This Web site (www.vtvnetwork.org/) offers background information on intentional communities and templates for creating your own community.

Aging in Community. This national directory of village networks (www.agingincommunity.com/) is a general resource site for information on intentional communities.

Chapter Notes

1. Principal Funds, *The Impact of Diminishing Wealth on Future Consumption: How Housing Wealth Affects Retirement Planning* (September 2008) (http://benefitslink.com/links/20080915-065182.html), accessed July 2009.

2. Principal Funds, p. 11.

3. Joint Center for Housing Studies, *The State of the Nation's Housing 2009* (Cambridge, MA: Harvard University), p. 13 (www.jchs.harvard.edu/publications/markets/son2009/index.htm), accessed July 2009.

4. John F. Wasik, "U.S. Home Prices May Be Lost for a Generation," *Bloomberg News* (May 4, 2009) (www.bloomberg.com/apps/news?pid=20601039&sid=aiiT.sNeq2YQ), accessed July 2009.

5. David Rosnick and Dean Baker, *The Wealth of the Baby Boom Cohorts After the Collapse of the Housing Bubble* (Washington, DC: Center for Economic and Policy Research, February 2009) (www.cepr.net/index.php/publications/reports/the-wealth-of-the-baby-boom-cohorts-after-the-collapse-of-the-housing-bubble/), accessed July 2009.

6. Dowell Myers and SungHo Ryu, "Aging Baby Boomers and the Generational Housing Bubble: Foresight and Mitigation of an Epic Transition," *Journal of the American Planning Association* (December 2008), pp. 17–33.

7. Joint Center for Housing Studies, p. 4.

8. Jonas D. M. Fisher and Martin Gervais, *First-Time Home Buyers and Residential Investment Volatility* (Chicago: Federal Reserve

Bank, November 29, 2007) (WP 2007-15) (http://papers.ssrn.com/sol3/papers.cfm?abstract_id=1083724#), accessed July 2009.

9. MetLife Mature Market Institute and National Association of Home Builders, *Housing for the 55+ Market: Trends and Insights on Boomers and Beyond* (April 2009) (www.metlife.com/assets/cao/mmi/publications/studies/housing-for-the-55-plus-market.pdf), accessed July 2009.

10. Laurie M. Orlov, 2009 Technology Market Overview Report (February 2009) (www.ageinplacetech.com/2009TechMktOverview), accessed July 2009.

11. Principal Funds, p. 13.

12. Financial Industry Regulatory Authority, "Reverse Mortgages: Avoiding a Reversal of Fortune" (www.finra.org/Investors/ProtectYourself/InvestorAlerts/Retirement Accounts/p038113), accessed July 2009.

CHAPTER 10

How to Hire a Financial Adviser

"The nature of any human being, certainly anyone on Wall Street, is 'the better deal you give the customer, the worse deal it is for you.'"
— BERNARD MADOFF, convicted Wall Street swindler[1]

REMEMBER THE BO DIDDLEY song "Who Do You Love?" When it comes to financial advice, a better question might be, "Who do you trust?" Bernie Madoff's victims certainly wish they'd thought harder about that question, and the general cloud of scandal hanging over Wall Street these days reinforces the need to work with trustworthy—and competent—financial advisers.

At the same time, as boomers confront the challenge of retirement planning, increasing numbers of us see that we need advice—lots of it! Even before the economic crash, the knowledge gap about retirement was large, and the need for smart planning has only become more acute in hard times. Do-it-yourself planning certainly is an option, but a little help from a professional adviser can be well worth the time and money. The rationale for hiring an adviser is simple: Money spent now could make a big difference in helping you achieve a secure, happy future retirement lasting two decades or more.

The field of financial-planning services is growing quickly, and finding the right person is a big challenge. Almost anyone can hang out a shingle and dispense advice; planners may have any number of certifications or titles attached to their names, but none are required. So let's break down the various types of advisory services that are available and talk about how to interview and select an adviser.

105

There really are only two types of financial advisers: those who—by law—work for clients and those who really don't. The legal litmus test is *fiduciary duty,* which means that the adviser is obligated to put the best interest of the client ahead of all else.

Stockbrokers and broker-dealer representatives are not fiduciaries. Neither are financial products salespeople working at banks or insurance companies. They are self-regulated by the Financial Industry Regulatory Authority (FINRA), an industry-sponsored group. FINRA's regulations require its members and their representatives to recommend investments that are "suitable" for clients—a definition with holes big enough to drive a truck through. "I've tried to find a definition, and the best I can find is 'reasonable,'" says Sheryl Garrett, founder of a network of fee-only advisers that bears her name. Garrett also is the author of the *Personal Finance Workbook for Dummies* (John Wiley & Sons, 2007), which contains an excellent chapter on hiring advisers. "But the investment only has to be reasonable at the moment it is made—not next week or next year. And the definition doesn't cover where the money that's being invested came from. I've seen situations where advisers talked clients into taking money out of a safe, government-insured defined benefit pension and putting it into a risky variable annuity. That can fall within the definition of reasonable."

None of which is to say that you can't get perfectly sound advice from a nonfiduciary adviser. Just be mindful of the possibility of divided loyalty and conflict of interest.

Advisers who have fiduciary responsibility to you as a client are registered investment advisers (RIAs) (the one exception being in California, where brokers also have fiduciary responsibility, although many advisers and consumers aren't aware of this). These advisers usually are independent or work for small firms, and they're regulated by the Securities and Exchange Commission (SEC) or by state authorities. They're held to a fiduciary standard of care that says they must put the best interest of clients first—not their own commissions and fees, and not the sales objectives of an employer.

Many people don't understand—or don't care—about the difference.[2] The current structure of the financial services industry has also tended to blur the lines, with the emergence of financial superstores that offer both advisory and portfolio-management services through different divisions.

The Obama administration hopes to address the current confusion by extending fiduciary responsibility to broker-dealer representatives as part of a proposed Investor Protection Act. One key provision of the bill would amend federal law to authorize the SEC to require that broker-dealer representatives or stockbrokers and investment advisers be held to the fiduciary standard.

Compensation is another major dividing line. Planners are typically paid in one of three ways: commission and fees, salary plus bonus, or fee only.

➤ **Commission and fees.** This is the most common approach[3] and usually is referred to as fee-based. The adviser receives a fee for developing a plan but also receives commissions for selling insurance or investment products.

➤ **Salary plus bonus.** Discount brokerage firms and banks will compensate employees with a base salary plus incentive pay for bringing in new clients' accounts. Advisers may also get higher bonuses by recommending or selling certain products over other options.

➤ **Fee only.** Typically, these advisers aren't registered reps for any financial services company. Usually, they are self-employed RIAs or work for a firm of independent planners. You pay all the fees, but the planner has no bias toward any one product or solution. You'll find fee-only advisers working in three ways: hourly, through a flat fee, and by retainer.[4]

 Hourly. Advisers who charge by the hour are recommended for clients who need advice about a specific topic or two. They are also good for people who manage their own finances but would like a professional checkup.

 Flat fee. A flat fee covers a package of services such as an analysis of whether you're saving enough for retirement and investing properly. This can be a good option if you think the flat fee won't exceed what you'd pay for hourly services.

 Retainer fee. A retainer fee typically is calculated as a percentage of assets managed for you or as a percentage of your net worth. Use this approach only if you want someone to manage everything for you.

While we're on the subject of writing checks, the only ones you should write directly to an adviser are those that cover fees. Investment checks should always be written to a third-party custodian, typically a big financial-services firm such as Fidelity Investments or Charles Schwab. Third-party custodians provide an important check and balance against potential fraud; Bernie Madoff's investors would be much better off today if they hadn't written checks directly to Madoff's in-house broker-dealer operation.

Alphabet Soup

Financial planners can earn any number of professional designations from an array of private professional associations. The designations indicate that a planner has taken a specific course of training that usually comes with a specific continuing-education requirement. But the designations don't really represent any specific seal of approval. These are the most common designations:

➤ **Certified financial planner (CFP).** Awarded by the Certified Financial Planner Board of Standards Incorporated. CFPs can provide financial planning and advice on retirement planning, investing, taxes, estate planning, and insurance.
➤ **Certified Public Accountant (CPA).** CPAs specialize in accounting and taxation. They can provide overall planning, although they tend to bring a tax focus to the discussion.
➤ **Personal financial specialist.** This is a CPA with additional training in financial planning.
➤ **Chartered financial consultant.** This designation usually is earned by insurance professionals.
➤ **Chartered life underwriter.** These are insurance specialists.
➤ **Chartered financial analyst.** These are experts who usually provide investment and portfolio management for institutional clients, but some also provide advice to high-net-worth families.

The services provided by advisers vary widely, too, depending on their credentials, licenses, and expertise. Generally, financial planners cannot sell insurance or securities products such as mutual funds or stocks without the proper licenses, and they cannot give investment advice unless registered with state or federal authorities. Some planners offer financial-planning advice on a range of topics but do not sell financial products. Others may provide advice only in specific areas such as estate planning or tax matters.

Hiring an Adviser

When you engage a financial planner, treat the process as though you're an employer hiring someone to do an important job in your company. Start by assembling a list of at least three candidates that you'll interview in depth. Recommendations from friends can be a good way to start, but you still must perform due diligence. A good starting point is to check a planner's record at the Web site of the SEC or FINRA (see the list of Web sites in the Resources section for due-diligence information). Ask prospective planners to provide access to current clients who can provide references and discuss their experiences with the adviser—but only in a general way. Most clients won't want to talk about the personal details of their finances with you, and advisers are bound by privacy considerations. Also ask the prospective adviser to provide a list of professional character references. There won't be any privacy issues, and colleagues probably have a longer history or working relationship with the adviser.

In interviews, ask questions about the following topics: experience, client base size, compensation, loyalties, disciplinary record, investment philosophy, decumulation experience, preparation, trust factor, and range of services.

Experience. Always ask planners how many years they've been practicing, and hire someone with at least five years' experience—and preferably ten. If the planner has less than ten years' experience, ask about other professional experience that might be relevant to his or her planning expertise.

Client base size. A large number of clients may indicate a planner is successful, but this isn't necessarily better for you; if a planner works with a very large client base, then you may not have access when you need it. Find out whether you will be working directly with the planner or with an assistant.

Compensation. Be sure to understand how your adviser will be compensated—and how much.

Loyalties. It's critical to understand whom a planner really works for—you or a financial services company selling a product. If you're interviewing commission-compensated advisers, determine whether they work for a single company or represent a larger, balanced range of products. Plan to ask—specifically—whether the adviser is a fiduciary. Also find out if the adviser is a registered investment adviser with the SEC and in which states—and ask for a document called an ADV Part II, which will indicate the states in which the adviser is registered and other important disclosure information.

Disciplinary record. You want a planner with a spotless record. Ask candidates if they've ever faced public discipline for any illegal or unethical professional actions. You can attempt to verify this yourself at Web sites such as those operated by FINRA, the National Association of Insurance Commissioners, and the SEC. However, remember that only the most egregious violations are reported—especially with FINRA, which is a self-regulatory body.

Investment philosophy. How does the planner approach investment risk, and how will your portfolio be adjusted as you age or if your personal situation changes? Will you receive a written statement about the investment policies that will be used in managing your money? Will you be granting the planner authority to make investment decisions without your prior approval? What kind of annual return on investment is the adviser promising, and is that realistic in today's market?

Decumulation experience. Keep in mind that you want a planner who is knowledgeable about the *decumulation* phase of retirement—the time when you'll be spending down your resources. Ask potential planners about their experience transitioning clients to decumulation and the kinds of strategies and products they recommend.

Preparation. Look for a planner who asks you to bring all of your financial information to the interview. Time is a valuable commodity; it's imperative that both you and the planner make the most of your time together. If you decide to work together, you'll be able to get started immediately. At the same time, never allow an adviser to pressure you into making a decision or sharing your private information unless you are absolutely comfortable that you're hiring this adviser.

The trust factor. Do you feel comfortable with the person you're considering? Does the planner keep his or her promises to you? Is the planner consistently on time for your meetings? Does the planner meet your standards for a trustworthy person?

Range of services. Make sure to understand what a planner can do based on credentials and licenses. Most financial planners can't sell insurance or securities products such as mutual funds or stocks without the proper licenses or give investment advice unless registered with state or federal authorities. Some planners offer financial-planning advice on a range of topics but do not sell financial products. Others may provide advice only in specific areas such as estate planning or on tax matters.[5]

Resources

Finding a Planner

The following professional association Web sites allow you to search for an adviser by geography or specific areas of expertise:

➤ Certified Financial Planner Board of Standards (www.cfp.net/search/)
➤ Financial Planning Association (www.fpanet.org/)
➤ National Association of Personal Financial Advisers (www.napfa.org/)
➤ American Institute of Certified Public Accountants—Personal Financial Planning Division (www.aicpa.org/)
➤ Society of Financial Service Professionals (www.financialpro.org/)

Due Diligence

The following Web sites will allow you to find information on specific financial advisers.

U.S. Securities and Exchange Commission. The SEC maintains an online database (http://sec.gov/investor/brokers.htm) that contains information about most brokers, their representatives, and the firms they work for. Learn whether brokers are properly licensed in your state and if they have had run-ins with regulators or received serious complaints from investors. The site also describes advisers' educational backgrounds and employment histories.

The Certified Financial Planner Board of Standards. The CFP Board database (www.cfp.net/search/) allows you to confirm that a planner is authorized to use the CFP designation and whether a planner has been publicly disciplined by the CFP board.

FINRA Broker Check. The Financial Industry Regulatory Authority broker checker Web site (www.finra.org/Investors/ToolsCalculators/BrokerCheck/index.htm) offers a tool to help investors check the professional background of current and former FINRA-registered securities firms and brokers.

Preparation

The Certified Financial Planner Board of Standards. The CFP Board offers a robust Web site (www.cfp.net/learn/knowledgebase.asp?id=6) that contains information on how to hire a planner. The site also has an online toolkit (www.cfp.net/learn/pdo.asp) that can help you organize the information you need to bring to a first meeting with a financial planner.

Chapter Notes

1. Reuters, "Factbox: Bernard Madoff Quotes" (December 17, 2008) (www.reuters.com/article/topNews/idUSTRE4BG0C120081217), accessed August 2009.
2. Angela A. Hung, Noreen Clancy, Jeff Dominitz, Eric Talley, Claude Berrebi, and Farrukh Suvankulov, *Investor and Industry Perspectives on Investment Advisers and Broker-Dealers* (Santa Monica, CA: RAND Center for Corporate Ethics, Law, and Governance, Institute for Civil Justice, 2008), p. xvi (www.rand.org/pubs/technical_reports/TR556/), accessed August 2009.

3. Sheryl Garrett, *Personal Finance Workbook for Dummies* (New York: John Wiley & Sons, 2007).
4. Garrett.
5. Certified Financial Planner Board of Standards, "How to Choose a Planner" (www.cfp.net/learn/knowledgebase.asp?id=6), accessed July 2009.

Work

CHAPTER 11

How Working Longer Helps

WORK IN RETIREMENT? It might sound like a contradiction in terms, but remember that we're looking for ways to achieve financial security over a retirement that could last 20 years or more. One of the best ways to do that is to work just a little longer than you might have planned. Working for even a few additional years can pay a surprisingly large bonus.

Most people say they don't plan to retire until age 65 at the earliest, but this is one of those cases where words and actions don't match. More than half of Americans file for Social Security at age 62—the youngest age of eligibility. The normal retirement age (NRA) as defined by the Social Security Administration (SSA) is 66; but in 2005, 55 percent of men and 50 percent of women filed for Social Security at age 62, according to SSA data. Even more striking, just 10 percent of men and women waited until age 66 to file for their benefits.

Working until their NRA could have boosted income in retirement by a third, experts say. The reasons are simple:

1. Working until your NRA means you won't incur the early-filing benefit reductions imposed by Social Security.
2. During your additional working years, you can continue to contribute to your 401(k) plan, building additional balances that can be put to work in the market.
3. Every additional year of income is a year in which you don't support yourself by drawing down retirement balances.

"The usual pattern has been to work forty years and retire for twenty," says Alicia Munnell, director of the Center for Retirement Research at Boston College. "If you push back your retirement age by four years, now it's work forty-four years and retire for sixteen, so the ratio is three-to-one. That just gives you a much better chance to have a really secure retirement."

The decimation of retirement portfolios in the market crash is just one of the major reasons to consider working longer. Just as compelling is the fraying of our nation's retirement safety net—just at the time when we need it to support a population experiencing growing longevity. "We have a contracting retirement income system and increases in life expectancy," says Munnell. "That means people will need to stay in the labor force longer because it buys you a lot. That doesn't mean you need to work until you're 90—maybe just a few more years."

Fraying Thread No. 1: Social Security

Social Security is a key part of the safety net, but it will provide a smaller percentage of lifetime replacement income in the years ahead—down from 39 percent at age 65 in 2002 to just 30 percent at 65 by 2030.[1] Intentional federal policy decisions are one reason for this; Social Security's NRA already is being shifted gradually from 65 to 67 under Reagan-era reforms enacted in the early 1980s. Another factor will be rising Medicare Part B premiums, which usually are deducted from Social Security payments, and expected increases in taxes on benefits.

Fraying Thread No. 2: Pensions and Retirement Savings

Our declining pension system is another cause for worry. In recent decades, employers have been shedding defined benefit (DB) pensions to reduce their long-term obligations. These are the old-fashioned type of plan in which an employer makes contributions, manages the funds, and promises to make regular monthly payments so long as the beneficiary (and sometimes spouse) lives. The percentage of employees at large- and medium-sized companies participating in DB pensions fell from 84 percent to 33 percent between 1980 and 2003.[2] Many companies have frozen their pension plans and shifted employees over to tax-advantaged defined contribution (DC) retirement programs such as 401(k) accounts.

DC plans should be able to help people build toward a secure retirement—in theory. The plans include the generous tax incentive that allows employees to make contributions with pretax dollars that accumulate tax free until withdrawal. And many employers also make matching contributions. But in the real world. DC plans have been a disappointment for many retirement savers. The stock market collapse erased a great deal of value, with investors close to retirement age registering losses as high as 25 percent.[3]

The biggest single problem with DC plans has been employee participation. Only about 56 percent of all employees use them,[4] due in part to inertia and lackluster retirement-education programs among employers. Just as important, about one in every two American workers doesn't have access to a workplace 401(k) plan. These workers are employed by small businesses that don't sponsor plans, mainly because of the expense of administering and matching contributions.[5] The employer incentive to participate also is ebbing, as a growing list of companies reduce or eliminate their matching 401(k) contributions to cut expenses during the recession. Finally, there's evidence that workers who do participate in plans aren't equipped to make good investment decisions and don't seem to pay close attention to their accounts.

As a result, 401(k) accounts simply aren't getting the job done for too many Americans.

Fraying Thread No. 3: Health Benefits

As recently as 1988, 66 percent of large companies provided supplemental insurance coverage to retirees that filled gaps in Medicare such as prescription drug coverage or capped out-of-pocket costs. By 2008, the percentage of big employers that provided that type of coverage had fallen to just 31 percent.

Fraying Thread No. 4: Housing

Before the housing bubble burst, many boomers were planning to tap their home equity to support their retirement-income needs. Housing values nationally have fallen by an average of about 20 percent from their peak, and no recovery is in view. One option here is a reverse mortgage, which lets borrowers relinquish home equity in return for regular or lump-sum payments. But housing can't be counted on as a major source of retirement cash in the years ahead.

How Working Longer Helps

How big a boost can you get from working longer? Financial planners at T. Rowe Price have used Monte Carlo simulations to project some answers. These are simulations that can be used to model future uncertainty, and the analysis produces outcomes based on hypothetical probability. But the illustrations make the point—convincingly—that you can improve your chances for long-term retirement security by remaining in the workforce longer.

First, let's consider the impact of working and saving longer on your retirement income. Consider the example of a woman who is working full-time with an annual, fixed salary of $75,000 and tax-deferred savings of $150,000. Let's say that instead of retiring at 62, she decides to stay on the job for three additional years until age 65 and that annual inflation runs at a 3 percent rate. Let's also assume she saves 15 percent of her salary, or $11,250, for each of those additional working years. Down the road, those decisions will boost her annual retirement income from investments by about 14 percent per year. At the end of those additional working years, her annual retirement income, in today's dollars, would be 43 percent higher than it would have been had she retired at age 62. If she could sock away even more of her income—25 percent—the total increase in her income from her investments alone would be 60 percent.[6]

Factoring in the benefit of delayed Social Security benefits really adds rocket fuel to the projections (see **Table 11.1**). The SSA's formulas give our hypothetical worker a significant increase in income; every year she waits to file for benefits will yield about 8 percent more in payments (in today's dollars). That really starts to add up in the out years. "Delaying three years, from age 62 to 65, results in a 29 percent increase in the purchasing power of a retiree's Social Security benefits," says Christine Fahlund, a senior financial planner at T. Rowe Price. "Waiting until age 70 to start taking payments would almost double that purchasing power."

Table 11.1 The Effects of Delaying Social Security Benefits

Age When First Taking Benefits	Benefit in First Year (in Today's $)	Increase in Benefit over Benefit Taken at 62 (%)
62	16,248	0
63	17,628	8
64	19,392	19
65	21,036	29
66	22,704	40
67	24,684	52
68	26,688	64
69	28,704	77
70	30,744	89

Source: Social Security Administration.

Next, let's combine the impact of our worker's decision to work longer and delay Social Security (see **Figure 11.1**). This gives us the most complete picture of how working longer can help. By working until age 67 and saving 15 percent of her salary, her gain in annual retirement income from both Social Security and her investments combined will be 58 percent, or $1,000 more per month in today's dollars.

If working longer makes such economic sense, then why don't more people do it? Certainly, the economic crash is forcing premature retirement for many older workers. But even when the economy was in better shape, more than half of Americans filed for Social Security at age 62, so the recession alone doesn't explain the trend. Health problems that force retirement are another possible factor, and the boomer generation certainly is confronting problems that could prevent many from working: Rates of obesity, diabetes, and heart disease are rising, for example. However, the research by Munnell of Boston College shows that, on the whole, older workers are no less healthy than they were 40 years ago.[7]

Munnell thinks that early retirement incentives offered by many employers, along with the availability of Social Security benefits, often outweigh workers' perception of the long-term gains available from working longer.[8] She also thinks Americans take the cue to retire at 62 from signals sent by employers, co-workers, and even friends and family. "It's a cultural expectation," she says. "People just think they should retire, and it becomes infectious. We see our neighbors or our spouses doing

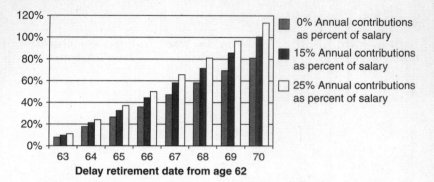

Figure 11.1 The Combined Effects of Working Longer and Delaying Social Security

Note: Percentages represent the increase in retirement income, in today's dollars, over the amount that would be received if Social Security were claimed at age 62.

Source: T. Rowe Price; reprinted with permission.

it, so we think we should, too." She also argues that the start of Social Security eligibility at age 62 creates an "easy out" for employees who don't find satisfaction in their work.

Working longer won't be a solution for everyone. For example, the odds for working longer are stacked against lower-income workers because they tend to do more physical labor and may not be in good enough health—or have the physical stamina—to continue working. Lower-income workers also are far less likely to have pension plans or significant retirement savings, so they are likely to be far more dependent on Social Security than any other income source in retirement.

But if working longer is an option for you, then think about staying on the job just a little longer. In the chapters ahead, we'll look at strategies for getting it done.

Resources

Social Security estimator. The Social Security Administration has built a useful online retirement estimator (www.socialsecurity.gov/ estimator/) that allows you to project your future benefits assuming different retirement ages. The tool is free and easy to use. Just plug in a few personal facts and your Social Security number; the site digs through your actual lifetime earning history and calculates your monthly benefit assuming different retirement ages. It's a useful decision-making tool and takes less than five minutes to use.

Social Security tables. The SSA also publishes tables online (www.ssa .gov/retire2/agereduction.htm) that show how much your benefits will be reduced with varying monthly benefit assumptions.

Retirement income calculator. T. Rowe Price offers a free online calculator (www3.troweprice.com/ric/ric/public/ric.do) that can help determine how much you will have available to spend each month in retirement and whether your savings will last throughout retirement. It will allow you to consider options for making up potential shortfalls.

Working pros and cons. AARP's Web site (www.aarp.org/money/ work/articles/return_to_work_after_retirement.html) offers a worksheet that can help you think through the range of financial consequences of going back to work.

Longevity. Life expectancy is the key to figuring out how many years of retirement you'll need to fund. Try the calculator at Livingto100.com (www.livingto100.com/).

Chapter Notes

1. Alicia H. Munnell and Steven A. Sass, *Working Longer: The Solution to the Retirement Income Challenge* (Washington, DC: Brookings Institution Press, 2008), p. 3.
2. Employee Benefit Research Institute, *EBRI Databook on Employee Benefits*, Chapter 10: Aggregate Trends in Defined Benefit and Defined Contribution Retirement Plan Sponsorship, Participation, and Vesting (Washington, DC: EBRI, 2009) (www.ebri.org/ publications/books/index.cfm?fa=databook), accessed June 2009.
3. Jack VanDerhei, "The Impact of the Recent Financial Crisis on 401(k) Account Balances," *EBRI Research Brief* No. 326 (February 2009) (www.ebri.org/publications/ib/index.cfm?fa=ibDisp&content _id=4192), accessed June 2009.
4. Dallas Salisbury, Employee Benefit Research Institute, "Boomer Bust? Securing Retirement in a Volatile Economy," testimony before the U.S. Senate Special Committee on Aging, February 25, 2009 (http://aging.senate.gov/events/hr204ds.pdf), accessed June 2009.

5. The Retirement Security Project, *Automatic IRAs: Extending Retirement Saving Opportunities to 75 Million More American Workers* (Washington, DC: Pew Charitable Trusts, Georgetown University Public Policy Institute, and The Brookings Institution, February 2007) (www.retirementsecurityproject.org/pubs/File/RSP_AutoIRAv12.pdf), accessed June 2009.

6. T. Rowe Price, *Working Longer and Other Ways to Optimize Retirement Income* (www.troweprice.com/gcFiles/pdf/2A41.pdf?src=Media_Near_or_In_Retirement&scn=Articles), accessed June 2009.

7. Munnell and Sass, p. 17.

8. Munnell and Sass, p. 59.

CHAPTER 12

The Fifty-Plus Job Market
Good News, Bad News

BY NOW, I HOPE you agree that working past traditional retirement age is critical to improving your long-term retirement security. Now for the real challenge: finding work—or keeping it.

At best, the employment outlook for older workers is mixed. Employers will say they value older workers' experience, knowledge, and loyalty, and it's clear that veteran employees are prized in some fields. But it's just as clear that employment security is eroding for older workers and that age discrimination is a major hurdle to finding a job or staying employed.

The Good News

Even in a tough economy, older workers are valued in some industries. For example, technology-oriented companies that depend on experienced scientists and engineers are very worried about brain drain. More than 50 percent of U.S. engineers and scientists are age 50 or older, and one recent global study showed that 3 million scientific, technical, engineering, and mathematically based jobs go unfilled.[1] Companies are scrambling to implement retention programs aimed at keeping these high-value-knowledge workers on the job as long as possible. Some offer flexible work arrangements that help accommodate the changing lifestyle needs of older employees.

One company, YourEncore, recruits professionals with scientific, engineering, and medical backgrounds to work on part-time consulting projects; the business was founded in 2003 by three blue-chip corporations—Procter & Gamble, Eli Lilly, and Boeing—to address brain drain issues in their own workforces. YourEncore helps plug the gaps by assembling consulting teams of already-retired experts to work on short-term consulting projects for client companies. "The preponderance of scientists and engineers in our country are boomers," says Brad Lawson, YourEncore's president and chief executive officer. "The companies that rely on them are worried about their retirement and the loss of knowledge that goes with it." In the aerospace and defense industry, for example, about 25 percent of all employees were eligible to retire in 2008,[2] and the United States isn't producing enough young engineering graduates to replace those who leave.

What if you're not a rocket scientist? Surveys suggest that many employers do value the loyalty, experience, and reliability of older workers. Some employers also say older workers are more productive and that their higher productivity offsets their higher compensation and benefit expenses.[3] One study, for example, attempted to quantify productivity and cost advantages of retaining and hiring older workers by showing that turnover and training costs can exceed 50 percent of a worker's annual salary—and that compensation and benefit costs for older workers weren't much higher than for younger people.[4]

The jobless rate for older workers has been lower than average even during the recession. In July 2009, for example, the jobless rate for workers age 55 to 64 and older was 7.2 percent—much lower than the 9.5 percent unemployment rate for the nation as a whole.

Another bit of good news is the shift away from physical work in the U.S. labor market—a trend that benefits older white-collar workers who want to stay on the job. The percentage of workers in blue-collar occupations fell from about 36 percent in 1971 to 24 percent in 2007, while the percentage of people in management, professional, and service occupations increased greatly (from 63 percent to 76 percent).[5]

Where are the most hospitable employers for workers 50 years of age and older? One hint can be found in AARP's annual award for the Best Employers for Workers Over 50. The award offers a snapshot of the most age-friendly large employers in the country and points toward age-friendly industry groups. AARP has been bestowing the awards since 2001, and the winner's circle usually is crowded with health-care companies, higher educational institutions, and manufacturing corporations with progressive reputations. A smattering of financial services companies has made the list, too.[6] The selection criteria include

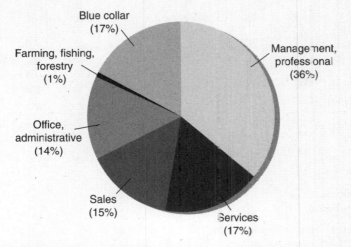

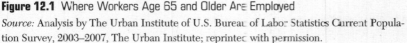

Figure 12.1 Where Workers Age 65 and Older Are Employed

Source: Analysis by The Urban Institute of U.S. Bureau of Labor Statistics Current Population Survey, 2003–2007, The Urban Institute; reprinted with permission.

recruiting practices, opportunities for on-the-job training, education and career development, flexible work arrangements, and employee and retiree benefits such as pensions.

One group of researchers at the Urban Institute—a Washington, DC, think tank that studies issues related to aging—tried a different tack. The researchers decided to identify the most promising areas of opportunity for older workers by analyzing industries expected to experience rapid growth in the coming years and then cross-matching them with fields that will experience high turnover because of retirement (see **Table 12.1**).

Many of the fastest-growing opportunities are expected to be in helping professions—teaching, social work, health care, and counseling. You can learn more about launching a second career in these areas in Chapter 16, which discusses encore careers.

The Bad News

Underneath some of the more optimistic numbers are some hard truths about the job market for older workers.

Unemployment lasts longer. Although the jobless rate among older workers is lower than the general population, the length of joblessness

Table 12.1 Twenty of the Fastest-Growing Occupations with Above-Average Shares of Worker Age 55 and Older

Occupation	Employment, 2007	Projected 10-Year Growth (%)	Share of Occupation's Workforce Age 55+ (%)
Personal and home care aides	794,846	50.7	23.4
Personal financial advisers	343,170	40.9	18.8
Veterinarians	66,824	35.5	22.4
Social and community service managers	340,736	24.6	24.4
Miscellaneous entertainment attendants and related workers	163,717	23.8	21.1
Surveyors, cartographers, and photogrammetrists	42,128	23.6	16.9
Environmental scientists and geoscientists	102,766	23.6	20.2
Registered nurses	2,608,762	23.4	17.9
Animal trainers	45,072	23.3	23.0
Instructional coordinators	24,165	23.3	32.0
Locksmiths and safe repairers	25,047	23.1	25.4
Postsecondary teachers	1,357,642	22.8	27.0
Archivists, curators, and museum technicians	56,396	22.2	24.7
Social workers	728,481	22.2	17.5
Management analysts	662,978	22.0	26.5
Pharmacists	229,830	21.8	21.4
Counselors	707,527	21.4	18.2
Business operation specialists, all other	100,367	20.9	18.8
Brokerage clerks	3,831	20.5	29.5
Religious workers, all other	109,127	20.5	32.5

Source: Analysis by The Urban Institute of U.S. Bureau of Labor Statistics Current Population Survey, 2003–2007, The Urban Institute; reprinted with permission.

is much higher for older workers. Unemployed workers age 45 or older required an average of 22.2 weeks to find new work in 2008, compared with 16.2 weeks for younger workers.[7]

Identifying an Age-Friendly Employer

Helen Dennis is one of the nation's top experts on aging, employment, and retirement. She consults with businesses on issues related to older workers and is the coauthor of *Project Renewment: The First Retirement Model for Career Women* (Scribner, 2008), an exploration of the midlife identity struggles facing career women.

Dennis says employer attitudes toward older workers vary greatly by industry, but she adds that most employers are simply looking for the best skills and performance at the best price. "It's easy to get preoccupied with age, but employers are looking at a more complex set of requirements. Can you do the job? Will you be my biggest return on investment among the candidates I'm considering? Do you understand the company's core values and goals for the short and long term? How can you help the company reach those goals?"

Dennis advises older job applicants to assess the age friendliness of potential employers by looking at the following factors.

➤ **Recruiting process.** Is an employer actively reaching out to older workers?

➤ **Marketing signals.** Does the employer portray older workers in its marketing and advertising materials?

➤ **Training opportunities.** Does the employer provide opportunities for continued learning and retraining on the job?

➤ **Benefits.** Does the employer offer benefits such as elder care and continuing education outside the workplace?

➤ **Advancement.** Is there a clear track record at the company of advancement for older workers?

The effect of a layoff is more profound. When older workers lose their jobs, they face the reality that they may not work again full-time, a blow that can wreck even carefully laid retirement plans. Household wealth typically takes a hit up to 23 percent for single people and 19 percent for married couples.[8]

Earnings shrink. Even when older workers do land new jobs, they typically experience a steep drop in income and benefits. Wages for people who take new jobs in their fifties fall by a median of 57 percent, and 25 percent lose their health insurance.[9]

Age discrimination is routine. It's illegal for employers to discriminate based on age in hiring and firing practices under the Age Discrimination in Employment Act of 1967. But it's widely acknowledged to be a factor in job loss and hiring practices—something that should be obvious to even a casual reader of newspapers, which routinely run articles about laid-off older workers.

In 2008, age-discrimination claims related to layoffs filed with the Equal Employment Opportunity Commission were at a record high, up 29 percent from 2007.[10]

And even employers recognized for progressive hiring policies agree that workplace age discrimination is a key obstacle for older workers. The U.S. Government Accountability Office (GAO) convened a conference in 2006 on the challenges facing older workers that included executives from AARP's ranking of best employers. The conference's final report concluded that workplace culture and employer perceptions can be unfriendly to older workers, and it stated that many companies "have not learned to place high value on their experienced workers, and they do not understand that much of their organization's intellectual capital and institutional memory can reside within their older employees."[11]

Some employers do tend to worry that older workers are less productive, less healthy, and more resistant to change. They also worry about cost issues, including health care, total compensation, and training. "Employers perceive that older workers cost more from a training perspective," the GAO reported. "For example, some participants stated that younger workers may have better computer and other technological skills. Also, employers are concerned about investing in training older workers because they may retire before the company recovers its training investment."[12]

Beyond discrimination, many employers are just indifferent to older workers' desire to stay on the job longer. One survey that presented employers with a range of steps they might take to help improve the retirement security of older workers found a "lukewarm" response to the idea of working a few additional years.[13]

Working past age 50 isn't a hopeless cause—far from it. But it's important to approach the employment market with a sense of realism. Knowing what you're up against is half the battle. In the next chapter, we'll talk about strategies for employment success.

Chapter Notes

1. Edward E. Gordon, "The 2010 Surprise," *Employee Benefits News* (September 1, 2009) (http://ebn.benefitnews.com/news/the-2010 -surprise-2681528-1.html?ET=ebnbenefitnews:e314:1673102a:&st= email), accessed November 2009.

2. Joseph C. Anselmo, "Baby Boomer Retirements Could Trigger A&D Engineering Crisis," *Aviation Week* (February 4, 2007) (www .aviationweek.com/aw/generic/story_channel.jsp?channel= comm&id=news/aw020507p1.xml), accessed May 2009.

3. Alicia H. Munnell, Steven A. Sass, and Mauricio Soto, *Employer Attitudes Toward Older Workers: Survey Results*. Work Opportunities for Older Americans Series 3 (Chestnut Hill, MA Center for Retirement Research at Boston College, 2006).

4. Towers Perrin, *The Business Case for Workers Age 50+* (Washington, DC: AARP, December 2005).

5. Gordon B. T. Mermin, Richard W. Johnson, and Eric J. Toder, *Will Employers Want Aging Boomers?* (Washington, DC: Urban Institute, July 2008).

6. AARP, Best Employers for Workers Over 50 (annual award by AARP) (www.aarp.org/money/work/best_employers/Best_Employer _Winners/), accessed May 2009.

7. Michael Luo, "Longer Unemployment for Those 45 and Older," *New York Times* (April 13, 2009) (http://www.nytimes.com/ 2009/04/13/us/13age.html?_r=1), accessed May 2009.

8. Richard W. Johnson, Gordon B. T. Mermin, and Cori E. Uccello, "Health Problems and Job Layoffs Crack Retirement Nest Eggs," *Older Americans' Economic Security* (Urban Institute), No. 8 (January 2006).

9. Richard W. Johnson, Janette Kawachi, and Eric K. Lewis, *Older Workers on the Move: Recareering in Later Life* (Washington, DC: Urban Institute and AARP Public Policy Institute, April 2009).

10. Jennifer Levitz and Philip Shishkin, "More Workers Cite Age Bias After Layoffs," *Wall Street Journal* (March 11, 2009), p. D1.

11. Government Accountability Office, *Engaging and Retaining Older Workers*, Highlights from a GAO Forum (Washington, DC: Government Accountability Office, February 2007), p. 4 (www.gao.gov/new.items/d07438sp.pdf), accessed May 2009, p. 4.

12. Government Accountability Office, p. 4.

13. Steven A. Sass, Kelly Haverstick, and Jean-Pierre Aubry, *Employers' (Lack of) Response to the Retirement Income Challenge* (Chestnut Hill, MA: Center for Retirement Research at Boston College, June 2009)   (http://crr.bc.edu/briefs/employers_lack_of_response_to_the_retirement_income_challenge.html), accessed June 2009.

CHAPTER 13

Six Rules for Job Hunting

"My son-in-law says I'm a dinosaur."
"Hey, don't knock the dinosaurs. They ruled the earth for millions of years.
They must've been doing something right."

THE 2004 FILM *In Good Company* generated a lot of buzz about workplace conflict between baby boomers and members of Generation X. Dennis Quaid plays a middle-aged sales manager for a national sports magazine caught in the pressure cooker of a corporate takeover; he finds himself working for an overcaffeinated Gen X boss (Topher Grace) who thinks Quaid is irrelevant and pushes him aside. Before it's all over, the Gen X boss calms down, embraces Quaid's boomer values, and moves to Los Angeles to jog on the beach. Quaid gets his old job back, and happy endings are shared all around.

Too bad we can't all have the Hollywood finish to our career stories. The job market is challenging for everyone in tough economic times, and it presents special challenges for anyone age 50 or older. What are the best strategies for finding a job? And, if you're still employed, what can you do to keep the job you already have?

As we saw in the last chapter, some employers think older workers are less productive, less healthy, and more resistant to change. The negative stereotypes aren't completely off the mark. Human resources experts and recruiters say older workers do often bring a false sense of entitlement to the workplace and resist adapting to changing business conditions.

Burnout is a key issue, especially in the high-stress, tumultuous business environment many employees have faced for years. The burnout factor can make it very tough to stay motivated as retirement approaches. But if you're looking for ways to stay motivated, consider your alternatives. If you lose your current job, you probably face a longer-than-average search for a new position. And whatever new job you do find is likely to offer lower pay and less generous benefits than your old position. Feeling motivated yet?

"Older workers need to take their best shot at keeping the job they have," says human resources expert Helen Dennis. "The best way to do that in this climate is by demonstrating that you are indispensable and by helping to increase revenue or cut expense. Show that you are well-informed, have relevant skills, and that you are innovative and creative . . . that you understand your employer's core values and . . . short and long-term goals."

It may seem obvious, but if you've got a job, *keep it if you can.*

Job Hunting

Let's say the charmed Dennis Quaid ending just isn't happening for you—or you're already out of work. It's time to roll up your sleeves and get ready for the challenge of finding new work in the worst economy since the Great Depression. It's a tough assignment, but not impossible. It's important to be realistic about the obstacles—and to focus on aspects of the situation that you can control. I've surveyed dozens of recruiting managers and human resources executives for their tips on 50-plus job hunts, and there's a consensus that older job hunters can succeed if they're flexible, focused on the prospective employer's needs, and willing to update their skills.

One important caveat: We're not really talking here about a single market of older job hunters. Hiring managers look at job candidates in their fifties differently than someone in their mid-sixties. "There is a consensus among boomer job coaches and employment experts that by age 58 it becomes very difficult, though not impossible, to find full-time positions with benefits, particularly in large organizations," writes Dr. David DeLong, an organizational behavior expert who published a major research report on the 50-plus job market for the MetLife Mature Market Institute in 2009. In fact, DeLong's research found that 42 percent of workers age 66 to 70 were self-employed.[1]

With that background, let's consider the key rules of the road in the midlife job search.

Rule No. 1: Package Yourself as a Solution

"The most important thing in getting a job after 50 is to understand why anyone would hire you," says Scott Kane, founder of Gray Hair Management, a career network and coaching organization for senior-level job seekers. "There's one common reason people get hired—when the hiring manager sees the candidate as the solution to their problem."

Kane says older job seekers often spend too much time talking about themselves in job interviews—narrating their résumés in too much detail and even showing off the battle scars inflicted by unjust former bosses. He urges job candidates to leave attitudes at the door. Instead, go into interviews prepared to listen and understand the prospective employer's current situation and issues. Research the company thoroughly in advance. You're there to find a way to match the employer's problems with your own experience and to portray yourself as a solution. "Don't whine about your last company, your financial situation, your health, or your children," adds J. P. Stein, a career coach and human resources consultant. "Employers really don't care. They are interested in generating more revenue, not in providing you with counseling. I know that sounds tough, but it's the real world. Companies may have a mission statement that says employees are their most important asset, but when push comes to shove, the company's bottom line is how they determine if they are a successful company or not."

When you have deep professional experience, there's a temptation to show off your skills and knowledge and to share your experience in great detail. That can be a turnoff, especially if your prospective employer is much younger. "It's important to share your relevant skills, but how you present yourself is equally important," says Tom Mann, a marketing consultant specializing in the 50-plus market. "Show that you're not only brilliant, but fun. Remember, Gen Y doesn't want to feel like they're working with their mom or dad."

Likewise, be careful not to give out the "been there, done that" vibe. "I see this all the time in experienced people," says one recruiter. "You need to appear excited about everything, no matter that you've been doing it for 30 years and can now do it with your eyes closed." And don't assume that just because you are older than your peers, you know more than they do. Demonstrate that you value what younger people bring to the table.

Put another way, approach the prospective employer as though you are a consultant who is there to solve the company's problem. Tom Hoglund, a partner with Accenture, the global consulting firm, takes this notion one step further. "Spend less of your time looking at open positions and more of your time creating a position. Look at the companies that need your expertise. Get a personal introduction to a leader using the extensive network you've built over your career. Schedule some face time to talk about what they're trying to accomplish. Listen a lot, but also tell them how you could help them. It worked for me, and I love what I'm doing."

Tom and I worked closely together in the 1990s at Arthur Andersen, the now-defunct global audit and consulting firm. At Andersen, Tom developed deep expertise in the field of knowledge management— the use of processes and technology to help organizations manage and leverage what they know in their businesses. After Andersen crashed and burned in the Enron scandal in 2001, Tom worked for a couple of years at a large publicly held technology company, but he wasn't happy there and found that he missed the culture of a large consulting firm.

At age 50, he was asking himself where he wanted to go next. He decided to try landing at Accenture, the former consulting arm of Arthur Andersen. He studied up on the organization and learned that Accenture had no formal practice group focused on knowledge management. But he did find two Accenture partners who worked in related areas.

The next step was finding a good route into the company. Tom identified a retired Accenture partner who made introductions that led to a face-to-face meeting. "The partner I met with admitted that they did get requests for consulting around knowledge management and that they could use someone at my level to coordinate and bring it together. I was able to create a position that fit my needs at a company I wanted to work for." That was in 2004, and he hasn't looked back. Most years since he joined, Tom has been able to double the size of Accenture's knowledge-management practice.

Even in a down economy, the create-your-own job approach is an appropriate strategy for senior-level people, Hoglund says. "With a higher-level job suited for someone over 50, companies often don't advertise those jobs or hire a search firm, since they'll charge a 30 percent commission on first-year salary to fill the job. So you can hit someone before they advertise the job and it isn't so competitive a field."

Rule No. 2: Skill Development Matters

Most baby boomers are comfortable with basic business technology—computers, the Web, e-mail, and mobile and smart phones. In fact, the criticism that boomers lack the technology skills to succeed is way off the mark if you stop to think about it. In the course of boomers' working lives, the digital revolution has brought the most incredible wave of technological innovation in human history—much of it invented and embraced by boomers. The list includes everything from personal computers and e-mail to cell phones, personal digital assistants, DVDs, and MP3 players.

But there are still some boomer Luddites trying to squeak by, hoping to finish their working years without getting fluent in technology. Only 36 percent of workers ages 55 to 70 have pursued additional training to help keep their skills up to date for their current or future jobs, according to the DeLong report.[2] Instead, many people become "prisoners" of whatever technology is present in their current workplace. "If it's Windows XP, we think we're up to speed generally," says DeLong. "It's easy to lose sight of the fact that the rest of the world is evolving outside your company. So when you enter the job market, it's likely that you're somewhat obsolete—either voluntarily or involuntarily."

If any of this sounds like you, it's time to get square with the world of work as it is today. If you don't like to use computers or send e-mail, then don't wear it on your sleeve or make jokes about it in an interview. Ask a tech-savvy friend to get you up to speed, or find a community college class that covers the basics.

"You need to know how to use the basic programs on a computer and have an e-mail address that sounds businesslike," says Tim Driver, chief executive officer of Retirementjobs.com. Adds Susan Ayers Walker, who writes about technology for AARP.org, "Know how to apply the latest technology to your prospective job. If you are applying for a sales job, know about mobile technology like smart phones and Web 2.0 applications and how to find hotspots for your laptop. If you are applying for a marketing position, then know how to use (Microsoft) PowerPoint, Excel, and Publisher and know how to start or post to a blog." Scott Kane adds that it's important to understand the subtle points of e-mail etiquette.

Concludes DeLong: "The problem for the 55-year-old is that a gap in technology knowledge is a quick way for a hiring manager to screen you out. If you go into an interview and a 40-year-old manager comments that he couldn't find you on LinkedIn, and you say 'What's LinkedIn?' you've knocked yourself out of the running. I'm not advocating that older workers need to make technology central to their lives, but they do need to be fluent in all the latest office and social networking technology. You've got to at least be conversational."

Rule No. 3: Network, Network, Network

The Internet has introduced an impersonal element to the process of applying for work; most often, résumés are submitted online, where they are sifted and sorted into databases for key attributes the hiring company is looking for. In many cases, getting a response from a human being is the first—and biggest—challenge. That's why networking is such an important element of the job hunt; it's critical to bypass the machines and connect directly with people in the industry or company you're targeting.

Your offline networking should include attending as many industry and professional conferences as possible and using less traditional networks such as alumni organizations. But a good deal of job networking has moved to the Internet, and the best online networking tool for business is LinkedIn. If you haven't signed up yet, do so immediately.

LinkedIn is a free, global social networking Web site for business professionals, and it can be one of your most important job search tools. The site has more than 41 million individual members worldwide, with representation across a broad spectrum of industries and not-for-profit organizations. Listing the URL for your LinkedIn profile is a great way to signal potential employers that you're up to speed on the Web and social networking. More important, it's one of the best ways to build your network of contacts and access business opportunities.

Scott Kane's E-Mail Etiquette Rules

Most recruiters prefer to receive résumés via e-mail. That means your e-mail note can be the first signal that you aren't fluent in technology. Scott Kane is founder of Cray Hair Management, a firm that coaches senior-level executives on job searches. He's seen so many violations of the e-mail rules that he composed a list of top 10 e-mail etiquette rules for job searches.

1. Get a real e-mail address. Cutesy names like Slide2b@, Debbynooch@, and hottotrot@ tend to diminish the seriousness of your search. The closer your e-mail resembles your name, the better off you will be.

2. Don't share your e-mail address with family members. Get your own account with your own e-mail address. Sending a résumé with your spouse's or family's return address is confusing and indicates that you may not possess the technological skills needed to communicate in today's economy.

3. Your résumé and every other personal document should include your e-mail address.

4. Your résumé file should be a stand-alone attachment and not a zip file with several documents included. (Note: AOL generally "zips" all multiple attachments automatically.)

5. Always make sure your full name (last name first, first name last) is included in the résumé file name you attach to your message. For example, "Kane-Scott.doc," and not "resume2001. doc." When the receiver copies your attachment to a folder, it will carry your name on it so that it can be easily retrieved.

6. If you're not using a mainstream word-processing program (such as Microsoft Word), you will want to ensure that your document will open. You can do this by making it an .rtf file, or even a .txt file if you don't care about the formatting. Sending your résumé as a PDF file or an Excel spreadsheet is not a smart move because many receivers won't know how to deal with these formats at their end.

7. Always include a cover letter along with your full name and contact information in the body of the message. Don't include your cover letter as a second attachment with your résumé because this will only confuse things.

8. Do not send your résumé attached to a blank message. Because of the threat of a virus, it probably won't be opened or read.

9. Make sure that your reply address in your e-mail account is set up correctly. You don't want replies to you that are undeliverable.

10. Treat and use your e-mail address as you would your own telephone number. In the not-too-distant future, it will become the more common method of contacting you.

On joining LinkedIn, you create a personal profile of your career experience that serves as a sort of online résumé. The site compares your employment history with those of other members and suggests people with whom you may want to connect. There's another powerful contact development tool on the site that can upload all the e-mail addresses stored in your e-mail account; you can then sift through a list of people you know who already are on LinkedIn and connect with them.

Once someone accepts your invitation to "link in," you'll be able to view your new contact's profile—along with his or her contacts. If you notice that your contact is connected with someone at an organization where you'd like to work, then ask for an introduction—which can be done via the site. You can also see news updates on all your contacts and join member groups that share your interests or affiliations (alumni groups, for example).

The common criticism of LinkedIn that I hear all the time is that it's a waste of time and "you can't get anything good out of it." Don't believe it. I've been using LinkedIn for three years now; I don't spend much time on the site, but I have a network of about 250 direct contacts and thousands of indirect secondary and tertiary contacts with whom I can interact at some level. I've fielded numerous inquiries about possible consulting assignments and full-time jobs, gained introductions to key people in my field, and received solid advice in response to questions I've posed to my network on the site. I might even make the case that you wouldn't be holding this book in your hands if not for LinkedIn; networking on the site helped me land the literary agent who helped me land a publisher for *The Hard Times Guide*!

Rule No. 4: Make the Cultural Connection

Interviewers will make snap judgments about you based on your looks. If you dress or wear your hair in an old-fashioned style, then you could lose out on a job based on that alone. Invest in new clothes, get a new hairstyle, and find some stylish glasses. Some experts even advise getting rid of gray hair. Perception can be everything, and you won't get a second chance to make a good first impression.

"They say 50 is the new 30, so we can act like it without guilt," says Sheila Ellis, a strategic business development consultant. "Spruce up your wardrobe with the help of an in-store retail stylist. Look the part of the job you are seeking. If need be, get a makeover."

Make a point of showing younger hiring managers that you're not stuck in the past. "Be brutally honest with yourself," says executive recruiter Jim Stranberg. "Understand how you are perceived by others— the way you look, the words you use, the attitudes you hold. Clean up your act before you enter the market."

Rule No. 5: Second Verse—Not the Same as the First

Don't assume that you'll be able to find a job doing exactly what you did before and for the same type of employer. DeLong argues this is one of the most common errors of older job seekers—and one of the most fatal. "The older you get, the harder it is to replicate the job you had, unless you have a very specific skill that is hard to find," he says. "The average 64-year-old will have a hard time finding a job doing what she did at age 50 full-time with benefits. There's just been too much change in the business world, and employers likely will see her as obsolete." At the same time, older workers are likely to overestimate the value of their experience. "They assume that since they've been doing something for years, the employer is lucky to have the opportunity to hire them,"

Résumés and Age: Don't Ask, Don't Tell?

Should your résumé tip off employers to your age? This is a question you may want to finesse. On the one hand, there's no doubt age discrimination can hurt, but you're also not likely to win a job from an employer who doesn't view you as trustworthy.

There's no clear consensus among experts on the résumé age-disclosure question, but it's wise to make your résumé as "ageless" as possible. "Most folks don't realize that certain dates on their résumé hint toward their age," said one director of recruiting. "Making your résumé as ageless as possible will help guide the hiring manager into focusing on your abilities and skills for that particular position. For example, it's quite an accomplishment to mention that you've received a college degree, especially if it applies directly to the job in question. However, it's not really necessary to mention the year you graduated. Also, most employers don't really need or want to see much employment history beyond 10 years. This gives the candidate a better chance of getting a foot in the door for an interview."

Likewise, "bragging that you have over 30 years of experience on your résumé or in a cover letter" is not necessary, she adds. "Remember, the purpose of a résumé is to get you an interview—not get you the job. Therefore you do *not* have to put everything on the résumé."

DeLong says. "It's a turnoff to younger hiring managers, so what boomers need to do is work hard to frame their past experience as something that can be put to work [solving] the employer's problems—show them how your past is a predictor of future success."

Rule Number 6: Practice Interviewing

Art Koff is the founder of Retiredbrains.com, one of the most successful online job-board sites for older workers. If you haven't had a job interview in quite a while, Koff recommends doing what he calls a "practice interview" with a company you're not really pursuing for a job. "You don't want to go to your first interview in a long time with the employer you are really interested in working for and make easily correctable mistakes."

Art's other favored technique for breaking back into the workforce is to register with temporary placement firms. "They don't care about age but are more interested in your skills and experience," he says. "Also, if you get work through a temp firm it helps build your résumé for future work assignments." Temp projects are easier to get than full-time jobs because the tight economy has employers looking for ways to save money on full-time salary and benefits. When applying for a job, tell the employer you are willing to work on a project or temporary basis. Temporary employment could lead to full-time work.

Resources

There's no shortage of services that help 50-plus and retired workers seek out employment. They range from specialized companies such as YourEncore, which recruits scientists and engineers for consulting projects, to general job boards and offline coaching firms.

AARP job resources. AARP maintains an excellent page of job-hunting links and other resources for older Americans (http://bulletin.aarp.org/yourmoney/work/articles/job_search_resources.html).

Best employers. AARP's best employers' page lists the top companies for 50-plus workers (www.aarp.org/money/work/best_employers/).

CareerBuilder. This giant job-board site maintains a special section offering articles, tips, and job postings for baby boomers (www.primecb.com/).

Execunet. This network of senior-level retired executives can put you in touch with other professionals and recruiters (http://execunet.com/).

Gray Hair Management. This career coaching and networking resources site for executives and senior managers includes monthly face-to-face networking sessions (www.grayhairmanagement.com/).

Jobs4Point0.com. An employment service for the 40-plus crowd can be found at www.jobs4point0.com/.

LinkedIn. Can create your profile, connect with old and new contacts, and get introductions to possible employers (www.linkedin.com).

Monster. Like CareerBuilder, Monster maintains a special section of its Web site offering articles, tips, and job postings for older workers (http://content.comcast.monster.com/get-the-job/older-workers/home.aspx).

RetiredBrains. Job listings on this site can be searched by state or industry. Articles offer how-to guidance on employment in retirement (www.retiredbrains.com/).

RetirementJobs.com. This site identifies companies that are suited to older workers and matches them with employees (http://retirementjobs.com/).

Seniors4Hire. Post your résumé and what you're looking for as well as search for jobs (www.seniors4hire.org/).

Vocation Vacation. This company markets travel opportunities that allow you to "test drive" more than 125 new careers and work with expert mentors (http://vocationvacations.com/).

WorkForce50.com. This site offers job listings from hand-picked companies that are actively seeking employees 50 and older (www.workforce50.com/).

YourEncore.com. This company recruits retired scientists and engineers for innovation-related consulting assignments (http://yourencore.com/).

Chapter Notes

1. David DeLong & Associates, "Buddy, Can You Spare a Job?" MetLife Mature Market Institute (October 2009), p. 23.
2. DeLong & Associates, p. 5.

CHAPTER 14

Fifty-Plus Entrepreneurs
Launching a Lifestyle Business

MEET THE NEW BOSS: you.

Many baby boomers intend to keep working past traditional retirement age. Surveys show that about 58 million boomers plan to stay in the workforce well into their sixties. Employers won't accommodate all of them, considering the state of the economy and attitudes toward older workers. And many will want to leave the corporate world anyway because of burnout or an impulse to run their own show.

All those factors will drive a major trend toward boomer entrepreneurship in the years ahead. For some, that will mean launching full-scale businesses with partners, investors and employees, office space, and all of the accompanying headaches. But far more will start what Mary Furlong calls "lifestyle businesses."

Furlong is one of the country's leading trend watchers on marketing, baby boomers, and the senior market. Her first venture in this market was SeniorNet, a not-for-profit organization she started in 1986 dedicated to helping people 50 and older master computers and—later—the Internet. She followed that up in 1996 with ThirdAge, one of the first online communities for older Americans. She has taught entrepreneurship at Santa Clara University in the Silicon Valley and runs a consulting firm focused on the boomer and senior markets.

Furlong believes boomers will create a wave of start-ups in the coming years—but says many will be small ventures that allow their owners to mix work, play, and other pursuits. "Boomers want to earn income and do something they like to do, but they're looking for a balance," she says. "With people living longer, the question is, how will we finance the bonus years? Are companies really going to hire us to drive their digital marketing strategies at age 62? It's not going to happen—they want the 28-year-old who has worked for three Internet start-ups."

Solo businesses are by far the country's most common form of entrepreneurship. At the end of 2004, almost 20 million Americans operated businesses with no employees, and companies without a payroll made up more than 70 percent of all businesses in the country.[1] Many are started as limited liability or Subchapter S corporations, which provide the legal protections of incorporation but flow income back to the individual for tax purposes. Americans ages 55 to 65 are forming businesses at the highest rate of any age group—28 percent higher than the average for all adults. The business formation rate for people ages 45 to 54 also is higher than average.[2]

The trend isn't surprising. Boomers have been through the grind of managing companies—and being managed by others. They're more than ready to walk away from the politics and pressure of large organizations and budgets, as well as answering to boards of directors and shareholders. And some just want to diversify their sources of income beyond a single employer.

Lifestyle business owners don't always leave the industry they've worked in; many launch businesses serving the companies they once worked for full-time. "They're looking for a 'no muss, no fuss' kind of business," says Jeff Williams, principal of Bizstarters, a company that provides coaching and training to boomer entrepreneurs. In most cases, these entrepreneurs want to work from home; many are empty nesters, so they have extra bedrooms that can be used for the business.

Lifestyle businesses can be started without much start-up capital—a big plus in a credit-starved economy. Many small enterprises are bootstrapped into existence for less than $10,000, especially if they can be run from a home office. The Internet and other digital technology make it possible to operate a solo business with little or no support staff. A web of relationships supports these entrepreneurs, with other solo operators and freelancers providing services such as bookkeeping or marketing.

Although these businesses may not consume a great deal of capital themselves, they also may not generate revenue immediately. That means entrepreneurs need to maintain an adequate cash cushion to pay living expenses while starting up—about six months, on average.

My Lifestyle Start-Up

In 2006, I struck out to start my own lifestyle business, a small publishing and consulting enterprise targeting the information needs of 50-plus Americans approaching retirement age. I'd just finished a six-year stint working on media start-ups at Tribune Co., the Chicago-based publishing giant. My last project there was a magazine and Web site targeting baby boomers approaching retirement. That experience convinced me that businesses could do well targeting aging boomers, a huge future growth market.

I started by assessing the market. The nation's demographic trends all pointed to a big emerging market for retirement information targeting baby boomers. Throughout their lives, boomers have dominated and shaped America's economic, political, and social scenes—partly because of our sheer numbers. During the postwar years of 1946 to 1964, 78 million baby boomers were born; it's the largest generation in U.S. history and is now aging rapidly, with 10,000 boomers turning 60 every day. By 2011, the number of adults ages 50 to 69 will be roughly equal to the number of adults ages 30 to 49, according to the U.S. Census Bureau.

It was also clear to me that many of us would be looking for something far beyond the traditional retirements of previous generations. Boomers wanted to pursue new careers, have active lifestyles, and find ways to give back to society. I knew this from survey data—and from listening to my own friends talk about what might come next. But I also knew that most didn't have a clear idea how they'd make the transition.

So it was a big market with a clear need for information and guidance. The business I decided to launch, 50+Digital LLC, initially focused on publishing and consulting opportunities in the 50-plus market. Its activities include my work as a syndicated columnist, two wholly owned Web sites, and an equity stake in a third online business focused on the 50-plus market. Along the way, I added a second business division that designs, develops, and launches Web sites for not-for-profit groups.

Early on, a major challenge was staying focused. When revenue isn't coming in, it's tempting to jump at whatever comes along, including opportunities that aren't really related to the business you're trying to get going. If you're confident that you've identified a promising product or service and core customer market, don't tack on projects or sidelines that aren't complementary to that core idea. For me, that means all the content creation and publishing work that I do focuses in a single area: retirement information and education. That work can feed multiple platforms, including newspapers, Web sites, speeches, and even the book you're holding. The consulting work is focused on a single market: developing interactive tools for small not-for-profit organizations.

Going solo felt risky at first, but I love the independence and the fact that I no longer rely on any single employer for all my income. The biggest reward, however, has been disconnecting from the culture and politics of big corporations—where everyday life is all about career compromise. I've replaced that with work that I value and that helps others. In my writing, I'm able to connect with readers trying to address tough questions about retirement and aging. And in my digital consulting practice, I help small not-for-profit groups get their messages out, stimulate activism, and raise money.

Health insurance is a key expense to consider. If you aren't eligible to join the plan of a spouse, then you'll need to buy an individual insurance policy, which will likely be expensive and offer limited coverage (see Chapter 7).

Another View of Risk

The entrepreneurial route is a good fit for people with some broad experience managing a business, including some understanding of sales, marketing, and finance. You also need to be willing to work harder than ever and at all hours of the day and night. Finally—and most risky—you must be able to identify and bring to life a business where there is actual market demand. You also need to be comfortable with the risk of the unknown and the absence of a steady paycheck.

On the other hand, ask yourself this: How steady is that paycheck, anyway? We're living through a time when the pillars of corporate America are toppling like dominoes. Do you really want to put all your employment "eggs" in one basket? Or is it better to diversify your risk among a variety of employers—who become your customers? Do you want your future determined by corporate managers you may not know or trust, or would you be more secure controlling your own destiny? If you've had the experience of bouncing through corporate downsizings and mergers, then a midlife entrepreneurial move might just be the less-risky option.

If at all possible, get started on your new enterprise before leaving the world of full-time employment. "If you have the luxury of preparing for your start-up while you're still employed, do it by all means," says Jeff Williams. The steady paycheck, he points out, can help pay for equipment and furniture you'll need. When you have a job, it's also easier to obtain a home-equity line of credit that you may need to draw on later to fund your start-up, he notes.

The other benefit of starting while you're still working is that you can test out your idea by doing some transactions while you still have a job. "You can do a lot to get ready before you strike out on your own, while you're still getting a paycheck," says Terri Mauer, an interior designer and industry consultant based in Ohio. "Do your business planning and market research when you have a job. Is the business you want to go into something that will be viable?"

Finding the Right Idea

Start out by asking yourself what you're really passionate about—because whatever you settle on will occupy most of your waking hours and energy for the foreseeable future. Launching a business requires a huge amount of energy and enthusiasm; if you're burned out from years in the corporate world, you really need something that can restart your engines.

The Myers-Briggs Type Indicator®, for example, can help you zero in on your true interests. You can take these tests at most community college career outreach centers, and many outplacement firms use them, too. Chapter 15 includes more on Myers-Briggs, among other self-assessment tools.

Starting a Business in a Recession

Is it smart to start a business during a recession, when consumer demand and business-to-business spending is depressed—especially as a midlife entrepreneur? There really is no perfect time to start a business. If you believe there will be long-term demand for your product or service, then there's no reason not to get started in a down market.

Midlife also can be a perfect time to get going if you have the time and resources to devote to a business. "If you're an empty nester, your living expenses have stabilized and you can devote more hours to the business," says Anita Campbell, editor of Smallbiztrends.com, one of the best online resources for entrepreneurs.

Here are some other positives about starting up during a recession:

➤ **Expenses fall.** The expense of running a business declines during a recession. Suppliers cut prices, and fees also fall for services such as graphic design and bookkeeping. Corporate downsizing throws a lot of high-quality office furniture and equipment onto the market at bargain prices, not to mention office space. You can equip your business for very little money.

➤ **Talent is easier to find.** High unemployment rates mean plenty of people will be available to work with you, even on a part-time or contract basis.

➤ **Angel funders haven't shut down.** If you do need to raise capital to start your business, consider looking for angel investors— wealthy individuals who fund small start-ups. Sources of angel investing can include friends and family. An Internet search will often lead you to a local angel-investor membership organization or club that networks and shares investment leads.

➤ **Tough times weed out weak competition.** If your business has staying power, then you'll find yourself running in a more open field and with a great chance to position yourself for real growth in the eventual recovery.

➤ **The first customer may be your old boss.** Companies are laying off employees, but their need to get work done doesn't go away—so that opens up more opportunities to do work as an independent contractor. Your former employer could be your first customer.

Aside from interests, you'll need a business that matches your skills. A start-up may feel like completely unfamiliar territory; but if you've learned to sell, develop a sales pipeline, and serve customers in your previous work, then those skills will transfer well to your new entrepreneurial pursuit. Experience in marketing, finance, operations, and business development is invaluable. "Boomers have experience and a network, and they've navigated through situations," Furlong says. "They have energy and intellect, they have the Internet for research, and they want to be mobile."

Some of the most promising boomer business launches will be focused on providing services to the growing population of aging boomers.

Furlong sees plenty of opportunity in businesses related to financial security and longevity for an aging population and also for technology services such as "senior geeks" who help people with their computers and digital media. She predicts elder-care services will be another explosive growth category with plenty of opportunity for entrepreneurs—everything from in-home services to adult day care, new assisted-living solutions, and fitness classes. "Boomers have always been willing to pay for services, and we'll be inventing new ones as we age."

Taking the Leap: Steve Vernon

Some people start businesses later in life because they want to; others do it out of necessity following a job loss.

Steve Vernon is among the fortunate ones who made the leap to entrepreneurship on his own. He took early retirement in 2006 from Watson Wyatt Worldwide, the employee-benefits consulting firm, where he was a vice president and consulting actuary. At age 53, he left a solid, secure job to start Rest-of-Life Communications, a one-man show focused on educating people about retirement transitions.

"I had worked at Watson Wyatt for 25 years, helping large companies manage their retirement programs. I felt that was long enough, and I didn't want to be the only worker hanging on until retirement. And I saw that vast numbers of baby boomers weren't going to have a traditional retirement—they hadn't saved enough, weren't paying attention to their health and long-term care issues.

"Meanwhile, as an actuary myself, I could see the longevity trends and that there was a good chance I would live to 90. Did I want to keep doing the same thing I'd been doing for another 20 years? Or was I going to do something that gave me a sense of mission that I would be passionate about—a reason to get up in the morning?"

Vernon took the initial steps toward independence while at Watson Wyatt by writing two books about retirement education. That helped set the stage for a full-time move. He saw going into business for himself as a way to address retirement education at the individual level full-time and get a better work–leisure balance in his own life.

Vernon says he doesn't make as much as he did working for a big consulting firm but has adjusted happily by downsizing his life. That included selling the house where he raised his two kids and moving into a smaller, less expensive townhouse near the ocean north of Los Angeles in Ventura County, where he runs the business out of a home office.

"I had enough resources saved that I didn't need to keep up the corporate pace and I could do exactly what I wanted to do, which is to provide people with unbiased, trusted information to help them prepare for retirement. I saw a need in society for my expertise; my kids were through with college, my mortgage was paid, so I thought, why not?"

Vernon's business is focused on a workshop series, an e-mail newsletter, and a series of DVDs and books his company has produced on retirement education (www.restoflife.com). The business is positioned as an unbiased provider of advice because Vernon isn't selling financial advisory services or products.

Taking the Leap: Al Brown

Al Brown was camping out in the backyard with his 8-year-old son one summer night when a tough question popped up:

"Daddy, why do you have to leave home so much?"

Brown—a 20-year veteran of corporate purchasing jobs—had just returned from a two-week business trip in Mexico. And his answer— "It's my job"—wasn't cutting it. In fact, the follow-up question was a real zinger—and it would change Brown's life: "Why don't you just invent your own job?"

Evaluating Your Idea

Jeff Williams of Bizstarters lists the following factors to consider when evaluating your business start-up idea.

- ➤ **The excitement factor.** Look for an industry that will truly engage you. This is especially important for burned-out corporate refugees, Williams notes. "You don't want to sink your sweat and savings into a start-up only to find yourself on another treadmill."
- ➤ **Understand the income potential.** Can your idea generate enough to match your needs? How much can you comfortably invest? Consider that most new businesses need at least three years to break even—if they last that long. Don't put your overall financial security at risk to start the business.
- ➤ **Energy requirements.** Match the physical demands of your chosen business to your energy level. "A business that requires putting in long hours every day, or hard physical labor, may not suit those 50 and older, Williams points out."
- ➤ **Variety.** If day-to-day variety is important to you, rule out businesses that involve doing the very same thing for each customer. The idea here is to find something that will keep you passionately interested.
- ➤ **Technology.** Do you love or hate technology? "While most businesses require some computer use, consider the extent to which you'll need to use other technologies—like wireless gadgets, the Internet, and various [types of] software—to help you manage your business," says Williams.

Source: Adapted from "The Ultimate Boomer Business Start-up System," Bizstarters.com; reprinted with permission.

"I had to admit it was a pretty good idea," Brown recalls. Tired of letting bosses set his agenda and exhausted by incessant travel, corporate cost cutting, and layoffs, Brown was approaching his fiftieth birthday—and he was about to become a self-employed entrepreneur.

Seven months later, Brown had quit his job and launched Supply Mex, a one-man consulting firm in Chicago's suburbs that helps U.S. companies find and manage product suppliers south of the border. The business seemed like a logical way to leverage Brown's extensive experience working in Mexico, his relationships in government and industry, and fluency in Spanish.

The Franchising Option

The franchising industry trains a good deal of its marketing firepower on midlife businesspeople, and it's an option worth considering. However, buying a franchise isn't really an entrepreneurial start-up—it's a way of buying into an existing business system.

Buying a franchise is a substantial investment. You'll need to raise anywhere from $75,000 to $250,000, depending on the opportunity—and the choices are varied. The top-ranked franchise opportunities in *Entrepreneur* magazine's annual Franchise 500 ranking included restaurants, hotels, shipping services, hardware stores, and tax-advisory businesses.

When you buy a franchise, you gain a recognized brand name, a tested system of doing business, suppliers, training, and even blueprints for setting up shop. It truly is an "add water and stir" proposition for going into business. What you lose is flexibility. As a franchisee, you've taken on a partner that will receive a percentage of all sales and impose strict rules on business operations.

Jeff Williams of Bizstarters advises would-be franchisees to be brutally honest with themselves about independence issues. "When you look back over your working life, have you shown an ongoing interest in coming up with your own solutions to business problems and then put them into action? Be careful about franchising if you think you might resent paying a perpetual royalty to the franchiser, if you don't like taking orders from others, or if you'd like to continually tweak the way you do business."

Since launching the business, though, Brown has had to make some adjustments. "I started with the concept of helping companies find Mexican supply sources as a consultant, but what I found is that companies didn't want advice or consulting but a product at lower cost and higher quality. So I changed my business model—rather than consulting, I am selling virtual manufacturing. I quote the customer's product, determine which factories in Mexico are best suited to meet their needs, and produce it." Typical projects include machining of metal parts and sheet-metal fabrication.

Brown wanted to replace 80 percent of his previous salary with consulting income within 18 months of starting SupplyMex. His business—started in 2007—is paying him about 60 percent of that income. The economic crash has slowed his business, but he remains confident that outsourcing to Mexico will keep growing when the economy rebounds. And he reports that his work–life balance is better than it was before he launched.

Resources

National Association for the Self-Employed. This trade association maintains a phone-based consulting service for anyone interested in starting a business. You can pose a question at NASE's ShopTalk 800 Web site (www.nase.org/feeds/ShopTalk.rss) and get a callback from a professional business consultant about any question on your mind, ranging from tax and legal issues to business-structure options and regulation. The service is geared to members; joining for a year will set you back $120, but you can get one or two free consultations.

Community colleges. Some of the best—and least expensive—training for entrepreneurs can be found at community colleges (www.50states .com/cc).

Ewing Marion Kauffman Foundation (www.kauffman.org/). This foundation is devoted to entrepreneurship and small business. The Web site offers a large collection of resource material for would-be entrepreneurs.

Smallbiztrends (http://smallbiztrends.com/). This resource offers entre-preneurial trends and advice from small business expert Anita Campbell.

U.S. Small Business Administration. The SBA Web site (www.sba .gov/smallbusinessplanner/index.html) maintains a section with resources that can help you determine if entrepreneurship is right for you and assist with planning.

Self-Assessment Tools

Myers-Briggs. The Myers-Briggs Type Indicator can help you deter-mine your own work style and understand if entrepreneurship is right for you. The MBTI is available from a wide array of vendors, but you can take the test for a modest fee at www.personalitydesk.com/.

Bloomberg BusinessWeek. Small business consultant Gene Fair-brother worked with *Bloomberg BusinessWeek* magazine to develop a shorter quiz (at http://images.businessweek.com/ss/07/01/0116_quiz _sb/index_01.htm) that can help you determine if entrepreneurship is right for you.

Franchising

Entrepreneur. *Entrepreneur* magazine publishes an annual rank-ing of the top 500 franchise opportunities (www.entrepreneur.com/ franchise500/index.html).

Consultants. Three major consulting companies can help you con-nect with franchise opportunities: Frannet (http://www.frannet.com), FranChoice (www.franchoice.com), and the Entrepreneur's Source (http://www.theesource.com/).

Further Reading

Mary Furlong, *Turning Silver into Gold: How to Profit in the New Boomer Marketplace* (New York: Financial Times Press, 2007).
Jeff Williams, *The Ultimate Boomer Business Start-Up Guide* (http:// bizstarters.com).

Chapter Notes

1. Institute for the Future, *Intuit Future of Small Business Report; First Installment: Demographic Trends and Small Businesses* (January 2007) (http://about.intuit.com/futureofsmallbusiness/), accessed May 2009.

2. Ewing Marion Kauffman Foundation, *Kauffman Index of Entrepreneurial Activity, National Report 1996–2005* (www.kauffman.org/research-and-policy/kauffman-index-of-entrepreneurial-activity-2005.aspx), accessed May 2009.

CHAPTER 15

How to Hire a
Career Coach

THE PERSONAL UPHEAVAL ASSOCIATED with career transition can be monumental—especially for those who face an unexpected, premature retirement because of job loss. Setting a new course can be daunting; and if you're like most people, you won't have a clue how to get started. You may also feel a sense of urgency to "get it right" because this career move may be your last. It's important to take time for some quiet reflection and conversation about what should come next—something that many A-type personalities find nearly impossible to do. What's more, the people closest to you may not be the best advisers because they bring their own preconceptions about you to the discussion.

That's where a coach can help.

Career and life coaching is a burgeoning segment of the advisory field, and many coaches have developed specific expertise in addressing midlife transitions. But coaches are a bit like financial planners; anyone can call him- or herself a coach and hang out a shingle. So it's important to pay attention to the background, training, and credentials of anyone you consider for a coaching assignment. Fees vary, but a coach typically charges anywhere from $75 for a one-hour workshop to $200 an hour for advice to senior-level executives and professionals. Some advisers will provide a free initial consultation; if you sign up, most will expect a three- to six-month minimum commitment.[1] If one-on-one coaching isn't for you, then consider a career networking support group. A number of excellent fee-based and membership options exist around the country.

Here's a look at the main types of coaching services available.

Group Retreats and Boot Camps

A number of organizations offer short courses, retreats, or boot camps that can help you think through your career direction. Some are offered on university campuses and are affiliated with lifelong-learning programs and communities (see Chapter 18). A typical and well-regarded example is the North Carolina Center for Creative Retirement, which is part of the University of North Carolina at Asheville. The center offers a three-day workshop, Paths to a Creative Retirement, that can help lay the groundwork for a post–primary career transition.

Support Networks

Small communities have sprung up all over the country that function as career-change support groups; some of these are self-directed, and others are led by coaches. The biggest and most robust networks are not-for-profits organized by and for women; the largest is The Transition Network (TTN), which was started in the late 1990s by two New York City career women—Christine Millen and Charlotte Frank—who were confronting their own questions about retirement. They started TTN after realizing that no organizations existed to help women understand career- and life-transition issues. Today, TTN has 10 chapters around the United States and 5,500 members age 50 and older; it offers a range of education programs and peer support groups on a wide array of career and life subjects, and members pay dues ranging from $60 to $125 per year.

The relationship between organizations such as TTN and coaches is complementary. "People get referred to us by career coaches," says Betsy Werley, TTN's executive director. "Coaches work one-on-one with clients but also recognize the need [for clients] to get out, meet people, and have a network. You need to talk with people about what you are thinking, get engaged, and get feedback."

Men are somewhat out of luck here; most of the not-for-profit networks that exist are for women only, and similar organizations for men are difficult to find. "Women tend to address their issues by forming communities, and they are open to learning from one another," Werley says. She also notes that many of the women involved in TTN went

Career Camp

Aside from one-on-one coaching, a number of organizations have sprung up that offer short courses, retreats, and boot camps that can help you think through your new career path. Here's a sampling of programs that enjoy strong reputations.

North Carolina Center for Creative Retirement. The center is affiliated with the University of North Carolina at Asheville (www.unca .edu/ncccr). Its offerings include a three-day workshop, Paths to a Creative Retirement.

Revolutionize Retirement Boot Camp. Weekend retreats twice a year help jump-start the search for what's next (www.revolutionize retirement.com/retirementbootcamp.htm). Guided meditation and creative exercises help those approaching retirement or in transition to a new career.

Reboot Your Life. Small retreats held in locations around the country teach the secrets of arranging a job sabbatical in order to recharge your life (www.rebootyourlife.us/).

Bolles workshops. Richard N. Bolles, author of *What Color Is Your Parachute?* runs five-day workshops several times a year at his Northern California home (e-mail fivedayworkshop@aol.com).

New Directions. This Boston-based consulting firm (www .newdirections.com/) offers a new spin on outplacement services for midlevel executives and professionals.

Gray Hair Management. This organization (www.grayhair management.com/) provides career networking and coaching for senior-level job seekers.

Execunet. This network of senior-level retired executives (http:// execunet.com/) puts you in touch with other professionals and recruiters.

Five O'Clock Club. A national outplacement and career counseling network (www.fiveoclockclub.com/index2.html), the club has certified career counselors across the United States.

Marika and Howard Stone: Too Young to Retire

Marika and Howard Stone completed successful careers in the publishing and public relations businesses in the late 1990s. Rather than retire, they started new careers with www.2young2retire .com, a website advocating a new vision of later life that subsequently expanded to coaching and a training course for other coaches, social workers, and career counselors. Today 2young2retire Associates has more than 240 certified facilitators leading groups about their future possibilities in 37 states and 14 countries.

The Stones published a book about their work in 2004, *Too Young to Retire: 101 Ways to Start the Rest of Your Life,* and were named Purpose Prize fellows in 2007 by Civic Ventures in recognition of their work.

As is the case with most coaches, the Stones' vision for coaching stems from their own personal experience. "We thought we would do traditional retirement," Howard recalls. "We had bought a place in Southern California when I was just 56 and thought it would be a beautiful place to retire. There were mountains, the desert air was dry, and we could play tennis and hike.

"But I noticed something missing in the neighbors we met there in the things they said and the way they looked. I realized they didn't have anything going on, and that really scared me. That's what motivated me to start strategizing about what I wanted to do next. I had a two-year plan to learn coaching and move out of what I was doing, and the idea of 2young2retire emerged from that.

"Society needs older people to be engaged in every part of society in order to have a good future for our children and grandchildren," he adds. "And any work—paid or not—is the medicine for longevity and fulfillment."

through the women's movement in the 1960s and 1970s. "That was a formative experience of saying we don't accept the options being presented to women, and it transformed the workplace. Now those same women are transforming this time of life after 50."

Life Coaches

There are 17,000 coaches around the world credentialed by the International Coach Federation (ICF) who help people deal with everything from weight loss to parenting—and many specialize in career transition. Many of these folks have backgrounds in counseling, education, or human resources; they typically start the process with a self-assessment tool such as the Myers-Briggs Type Indicator to help clients zone in on skills, personality traits, and values (see **Table 15.1**). Expect your coaching sessions to be done in person or over the phone; some coaches even convene regular group teleconferences for clients. The ICF website (www.coachfederation.org/) offers a coach referral service that can be used to search for a coach by geography or expertise so you can query coaches who interest you.

Career Counselors

If emotional issues are a barrier to your next career move, then you may want to consider hiring a career counselor. Although they're not psychotherapists, counselors can help clients deal with problems such as a fear of failure, job-hunting anxiety, and lingering anger over a layoff. Counselors are licensed and regulated in every state except California.[2] The American Counseling Association provides a list of counselors at

Table 15.1 A Sampling of Self-Assessment Tests

Work Personality Index	Measure where you stand on 17 personality dimensions related to performance and workplace satisfaction.	www.psychometrics.com/en-us/assessments/wpi.htm
Myers-Briggs Type Indicator	Gain insight into your own personal work style and how to work more productively with other people.	www.personalitydesk.com/
Strong Interest Inventory	Get an in-depth assessment of your interests and how they line up against a broad range of occupations, work, and leisure activities.	www.personalitydesk.com/strong-interest-inventory.php

Source: Adapted from "Self-Assessment Tests" (www.whatsnext.com/content/self-assessment-tests), What's Next Media (http://whatsnext.com); reprinted with permission.

Reinvention Networks

Small communities have sprung up all over the country that function as career-change support groups. Some of these are self-directed, while others are led by coaches.

The Transition Network. This network for women (www.the transitionnetwork.org/) has members in New York City and chapters around the country.

Project Renewment. A West Coast (www.projectrenewment.com/) support network for women.

Life by Design. This Portland, Oregon–based consortium of educational, business, and not-for-profits (www.lifebydesignnw.org/) offers life planning, work, volunteer, and community resources to individuals 50 and older.

Too Young to Retire. Life transition coaching and training is offered through a network of coaches run by coaches Marika and Howard Stone (www.2young2retire.com/default.shtml).

Bizstarters. Coach, trainer, and author Jeff Williams specializes in teaching baby boomers how to transition from jobs to entrepreneurship. Jeff's program focuses on applying his book *The Ultimate Boomer Business Start-Up Guide* (http://bizstarters.com/).

WomanSage. Journalist Jane Glenn Haas leads this Southern California women's networking group (www.womansage.org/).

Coming of Age. This Philadelphia-area resource (http://comingofage .org/) for men and women has information on careers, volunteering, and educational and social activities.

Shift. A Twin Cities resource for men and women focused on job searching (www.shiftonline.org/).

Tempe Connections. This organization provides learning, work, and volunteer resources to 50-plus adults in the Tempe, Arizona, area (www.tempeconnections.org/).

the website of its affiliate, the National Career Development Association (www.ncda.org).

Resources

County and municipal employment offices, often known as *career one-stops,* offer career counseling, self-assessment, support groups, and databases of job listings. Go to www.careeronestop.org to find the nearest resource center.

International Coach Federation. The ICF Web site (www.coach federation.org/) includes a coaching referral service that enables prospective clients to search for a coach by geographical area and expertise and then send an anonymous query to as many as 100 coaches.

Retirement Options. This organization (www.retirementoptions.com/ FindACoach.asp) has trained coaches across the country and around the world.

The Life Planning Network (LPN). The LPN is a community of professionals from diverse fields who share a commitment to providing a broad spectrum of life-planning services and resources for what some professions call the third age. Based in Boston, LPN's influence is expanding as satellite groups are forming in other cities. The member list can be viewed at www.lifeplanningnetwork.org/ find-consultant.htm.

Next Chapter Initiative. These community coalitions (www.civic ventures.org/nextchapter/overview.cfm) are working to help people in the second half of life set a course, connect with peers, and find pathways to meaningful work and significant service.

Further Reading

Bernice Brattner and Helen Dennis, *Project Renewment: The First Retirement Model for Career Women* (New York: Scribner, 2008). The authors also manage a support network for women (www .projectrenewment.com/) on the West Coast.

Elizabeth Pope, *Career Change and Life Balance* (New York: What'sNext, 2009). This free e-book guide to coaching and advisory services is available for download at http://whatsnext.com/content/career-change-life-balance-free-special-report. The site also offers a free database of career and life coaches that is searchable by geography and expertise. Full disclosure: I am a partner in What'sNext LLC and edited Elizabeth's guide.

Gail Rentsch, *Smart Women Don't Retire—They Break Free: From Working Full-Time to Living Full-Time* (New York: Springboard Press, 2008).

William Stone, "Real Work Gives Real Meaning to an Unpaid Charity Job," *Chronicle of Philanthropy* (June 28, 2007) (http://philanthropy.com/free/articles/v19/i18/18004101.htm). In this article, a retired attorney tells the story of his shift into a job as an unpaid executive at a not-for-profit organization.

Chapter Notes

1. Elizabeth Pope, *Career Change and Life Balance* (New York: What'sNext, 2009), p. 15 (http://whatsnext.com/content/career-change-life-balance-free-special-report).
2. Pope, p. 17.

Living

CHAPTER 16

Making a Difference
Encore Careers

BEFORE THE ECONOMY CRASHED, millions of midlife adults already were starting new careers in fields where they hoped to make a difference—areas such as teaching, health care, and the not-for-profit world. The new economic realities will make career reinvention mandatory for many millions more who aren't ready to retire or who simply can't afford to quit working. However, the tough economy hasn't forced baby boomers to give up their dream of second careers with meaning; and retirement gurus have been struggling to label the trend, so far without much success. But one name has come along that I think works pretty well: the *encore career.*

The phrase was coined by Civic Ventures, a California-based not-for-profit think tank and incubator for social entrepreneurship cofounded by Marc Freedman and John Gardner in the late 1990s. Gardner, who died in 2002 at age 89, was a visionary thinker and leader on civic engagement, civil rights, and social reform. He wrote extensively on leadership and self-renewal, and he cofounded Experience Corps, the national organization that promotes and enables volunteer work for older Americans. Gardner also played a key role in creating Medicare when he served as secretary of Health, Education, and Welfare in the Johnson administration.

Freedman is one of the country's leading thinkers on how Americans can redefine the second half of life with a sense of social and in-dividual renewal—a notion Civic Ventures tries to capture with the brand name Encore Careers. A national movement-style community has sprung up around civic engagement for older Americans, and Freedman's organization is at the hub. The core idea is expressed in Freedman's book, *Encore: Finding Work That Matters in the Second Half of Life* (PublicAffairs Books, June 2007). Civic Ventures has further amplified the idea by funding innovative career retraining programs at community colleges around the country and with an annual award program called the Purpose Prize, which makes cash awards to social innovators age 60 and older. There's also a free online social network, Encore.org, that offers resources for career transition and a place for encore careerists to share ideas and compare notes.

Freedman sees the encore career as an antidote to the notion that baby boomers will be a drain on society's resources as they move into their golden years. Instead of ballooning Social Security and Medicare payments, he foresees a generation pursuing new work—both paid and volunteer—that allows them to make a positive contribution in later life. In fact, he argues that the entire concept of retirement is headed for the dustbin. "For the last half century, we've had a cultural vision of success in later life that focused on liberation from work," he says. That vision may have outlived its time—the result of financial need, greater longevity, and boomer lifestyle preferences. For example, one Civic Ventures survey found that more than half of adults ages 50 to 70 want to find ways to "contribute to the greater good" in retirement. The research also found that somewhere between 5.3 million and 8.4 million people ages 44 to 70 already are doing work that combines income and personal meaning with social impact. "It starts with the bread-and-butter issues of income if people can genuinely get greater security with well-paying positions that have benefits," Freedman notes. The encore career concept turns on its head the idea of retirement as a time of self-indulgence. It's not about satisfying your own needs, but thinking about ways you can leave a legacy and a better world for the next generation.

Where can you find an encore career for yourself? Let your imagination run wild. It can be found anywhere there's a clear social need that fits your passions and interests. But some fields have surfaced as clear early adopters of the encore career concept. And best of all, they're fields where the number of jobs is growing.

Teaching

A huge number of teaching jobs will open up in the next decade as a result of turnover and retirements. The Woodrow Wilson National Fellowship Foundation estimates the number of job vacancies in the United States at 1.5 million. It's a profession that appeals to the impulse for community service felt by many boomers, although the hard work of training to teach and actually getting into the classroom can quickly dispel any romantic notions you might be harboring.

But interest in teaching as an encore career is taking off, and so are innovative programs designed to help people make the transition. In California, for example, a shortage of more than 100,000 teachers is projected over the coming decade, with about 33,000 of the open jobs in science and math. A group of public- and private-sector leaders in the state came together to try to close the gap with the EnCorps teachers program, one of the country's most innovative programs for midlife career transition.

EnCorps is dedicated to increasing the number of much-needed math and science teachers in California's public middle and high schools. A network of corporate sponsors promotes EnCorps to employees nearing retirement, and the program has trained more than 120 teachers, who undergo a rigorous training process aimed at transitioning to a second career in education. An intensive application process seeks to make certain that an applicant is really ready to move into teaching, including a state-required competency test. Successful applicants then commit to 120 hours of training and classroom experience. At the same time, they take teacher-training classes through the California state university system. EnCorps also has expanded its initial focus to involve retirees at varying levels; retirees can apply to volunteer in a classroom, substitute teach, or get on the full-time teaching track.

The EnCorps program is modeled on a similar program launched in 2005 by IBM Corporation called Transition to Teaching. The company wanted to help employees fulfill their desire to give back to the community—but also help meet its own future need for scientists and engineers by funneling qualified teachers back into the schools. "We have incredible math and science professionals at IBM," said Robin Willner, IBM's vice president of global community initiatives.

Shifting from Aerospace to a High School Classroom

When Sharon White was growing up, her career goal was clear: "I wanted to find a way to make money," she recalls.

An African-American woman who grew up in Compton, California, in the 1950s, White pursued a career in business, acquiring degrees in accounting, business administration, and finance along the way. In 2008, she retired at age 61 from her job as a financial analyst at Boeing Corporation after a successful 34-year career in the aerospace industry.

As retirement approached, she found herself thinking about new challenges—and ways to leave a positive legacy. "I've done more than I dreamed I could do, because my dreams weren't that big when I was young. And I had help along the way from a lot of people, so you want to find a way to give back. I wanted to figure out where I was going next and how to find my passion."

White made the transition by enrolling in the EnCorps teachers program. White heard about EnCorps through Boeing, one of the program's corporate sponsors. She was in the first class of recruits to undergo a rigorous training process aimed at transitioning to a second career in education.

"I came across this by accident," White says. "Boeing sent out an e-mail about the program, and I thought, 'What the heck,' so I called. I don't know what I was expecting, but I completed the application process and the interviews. And I started realizing, this is something that really could make a difference at needy schools for kids. I spent all my life making money. . . . I'm not wealthy but that is what the process was. You get to a point where you start thinking, 'I want to find my passion.' That is what I was looking for."

White has found the training process very challenging, but worthwhile—and today she is on the front lines of education reform. She teaches algebra to ninth- and tenth-grade students at Locke Senior High School, a gang-ridden Los Angeles school undergoing a transformation as a charter school. "Don't let anyone tell you that midlife career changes or chasing your dreams are easy," she says. "They aren't! They are just 'worth it.'"

"They're some of the best-educated 50-year-olds to ever walk the planet, and they are trying to figure out what to do next. Many of them have a strong interest in education and volunteering and getting kids excited about math and science." IBM invests $15,000 in training for each Transition to Teaching participant. So far, 86 IBM

Teacher Transitions at IBM

When Jim Siegfried was an undergraduate student in the early 1970s, he wanted to become a teacher; but there was a large surplus of teachers at the time, and mentors advised him to look elsewhere. He went to work in the business world and spent several decades working in the food-service industry. Later on, he went to work in Texas as a manager in a customer support department at IBM, where he spent nine years.

But Siegfried had never given up on his classroom dreams. At age 51, he decided to start working toward a master's degree in teaching. He'd already completed a good deal of his coursework when IBM created its Transition to Teaching program for midlife career switchers, and Jim was accepted. That meant $15,000 in support to offset his tuition, plus the support of his supervisors and the freedom to take a leave of absence from work to do his student teaching. He was hired in the fall of 2007 to teach math at an elementary school in Arlington, Texas, and assigned to work with a classroom of children who were struggling with a state test that must be passed if students are to graduate to middle school. In his first year, Siegfried helped twelve of his fifteen students pass the exam.

"At IBM, thirty other people could do exactly what I did—I was easy to replace," he says. "Teaching has changed a lot of that for me. Especially at the elementary level, the students get attached to you, and you have a year-long plan for getting them on the road to success, so I hate to miss a single day. I have a sense of passion about my work—I wake up every day and want to do everything I can to go above and beyond.

"This is the job I was meant to do all along!"

employees in 19 states are studying to become teachers, and 14 graduates have been placed in schools.

Corporate-sponsored programs such as IBM's are somewhat rare, but there are plenty of other options for getting trained—a process that can take as long as three years but can be done more quickly through alternative certification programs. These include programs sponsored by governments, community colleges, and not-for-profit teaching fellowship programs. Certification requirements differ by state.

Health Care

The health-care sector continues to grow despite the economy's overall weakness—the result of our aging population and growing use of health-care services. For example, in one of the worst months of the recession—February 2009—hospitals and facilities for long-term care and other ambulatory care added 27,000 new jobs, even though employers overall shed more than 680,000 positions.[1] The health-care industry got an additional shot in the arm from the federal economic stimulus bill passed in 2009, which included $59 billion for medical research, prevention initiatives, and a national health-information-technology infrastructure.

The nursing profession faces an especially acute shortage of skilled labor, the result of the health sector's projected growth, expected retirements, and a shortage of training programs for new nurses. The number of available positions is expected to grow 2 percent to 3 percent annually through 2016, and one study projects a shortage of 500,000 registered nurses by the year 2025. There are similar shortages projected in the ranks of pharmacists and home-care aides. Positions also exist for people who aren't trained medical professionals—in music and art therapy, occupational health and safety, and social work.

The Federal Government

The U.S. government is legendary for its insular hiring practices, but now it's facing a major labor shortage in key skilled positions because of its aging workforce. The not-for-profit Partnership for Public Service has forecast that the federal government will need to fill 273,000 critical-need federal jobs through 2012. That figure is 41 percent higher than

Working for Uncle Sam

Uncle Sam wanted Ann Vande Vanter—and he might want you, too, if you're over age 50.

After a 30-year career as an accountant in the private sector, Vande Vanter was looking for a change. She had worked for several big global audit firms and corporations; the hours were long, but the pay was good and she enjoyed the intellectual challenges of dealing with complex tax laws in the United States and other countries. But about seven years ago, she found herself craving better balance between her work and personal life. At the same time, the accounting scandals at Enron and WorldCom were roiling the business world, shaking her faith in the value of private-sector work.

"What we were all reading in the papers clearly showed a lack of corporate governance. I got to a point where I wanted to use my skills and knowledge for the greater good of all taxpayers rather than those fortunate enough to own substantial shares in really profitable companies."

Vande Vanter decided to pursue a new career at the Internal Revenue Service (IRS), where she was hired in 2004. "The IRS has no interest in anyone paying more than their legal tax obligation; but I thought that since I had worked in public accounting and the private sector, I could bring a better understanding of the inner workings at corporations to IRS."

She currently works as the senior technical analyst for a division that focuses on taxes for large and mid-sized companies in the natural resources and construction industries.

"There's a tremendous difference in the work-life balance, and I've never worked with a nicer, more professional group of people. Most people here are very patriotic and feel that they're doing the right thing." Vande Vanter also found that, once in the door, moving around within the government was easy. She's in her third position at IRS in less than five years, having been posted twice in her native Texas and once in Washington, DC.

it was when the Partnership did its last federal jobs forecast in 2007. The areas of greatest demand include the medical and health field, security and law enforcement, and administrative positions, but opportunities exist across a wide range of federal positions.

The partnership works on an array of initiatives aimed at recruiting Americans to public service. In 2008, it launched an initiative focused on recruiting older workers called FedExperience Transitions to Government. The partnership is piloting the program with the U.S. Department of the Treasury and also envisions working with private-sector employers interested in helping their own retiring workers navigate toward encore careers. The FedExperience program also has a private-sector partner, IBM, which has rolled out a program for its employees similar to its Transition to Teaching program.

Traditionally, the federal government has tended to hire young people just starting their careers and promote from within. Although the hiring culture is starting to open up to more mid-career transitions, few people know about the opportunities. A study by the Partnership found that just 11 percent of older Americans are knowledgeable about government job opportunities. Red tape in the federal hiring process poses another big hurdle. Getting hired can take much longer than it does in the private sector—often as much as two years.

The biggest lure for boomers is finding meaning and impact in work, argues Max Stier, president of the Partnership. "Older Americans most value meaningful work in an encore career—they want to make a difference where it matters. There's just no better platform for doing that than in the federal government, whether it's global warming or globalization. The federal government will present you with some of the biggest, most complex problems at a scale that is bigger than you will find even at the largest companies."

Green Careers

Green careers have surfaced as a major area of interest for people steering toward encore careers. Environmental work is expected to be one of the fastest-growing employment categories in the years ahead, particularly as the United States undergoes major changes in energy production and consumption. A 2008 report produced for the U.S. Conference of Mayors predicted that the country could add as many as 4.2 million green jobs in the coming two decades. The 2009 federal stimulus act is a factor here, too: The legislation allocated billions of dollars to be spent stimulating green businesses, including $16.8 billion for energy efficiency and renewable energy, and nearly $1 billion for green-job training. The federal stimulus for green jobs will likely continue to grow with passage of further green legislative initiatives.

If you have specialized skills—engineering, for example—emerging fast-growth industry segments include solar energy and other renewable sources. But professionals without specific environmental job backgrounds—such as architects and project managers—also have skills that can be transferred with some retraining, according to Paul Hannam, cofounder of Bright Green Talent, an environmental talent search and recruiting firm. "Most of the jobs of a technical nature will take people without direct environmental experience and then retrain them," he says. "A good engineer can easily learn the skills. It's better to have good engineering experience from manufacturing cars, for example, than to be an engineer with a weak track record from the solar industry." Hannam also foresees strong demand for nontechnical people coming from outside the environmental field. "Every business needs accounting, human resources, and marketing people," he says. "The market is very new, so very few come with direct experience at green companies. The most important thing is to have a track record of performance and skills that can transition to an environmental business."

The U.S. Conference of Mayors report surveyed a range of green job markets and identified strong growth potential in renewable power generation, residential and commercial retrofitting, renewable transportation fuels, and professional services.

If you don't have direct experience in green business, then consider getting training or certification. For example, Leadership in Energy and Environmental Design (LEED) offers a certification program leading to a credential as a green building specialist. LEED-accredited professionals can advise on green building projects for architects, designers, and developers on environmentally sustainable buildings.

Another good way to get started on a green job is through online networking. An abundance of green business conferences around the country can be found through a simple Google search. You can also find many robust online discussion groups focused on green business at LinkedIn, the social network for career professionals.

Not-for-Profit Careers

It may seem like the business world is crumbling, but not-for-profits continue to grow—and they're facing a shortage of talent. Best of all, the not-for-profit sector is gradually waking up to the potential of encore career switchers from the business world.

Not-for-profits are hardly immune to the effects of recession. And they face pressure in maintaining their fundraising as donor wallets get thinner. The stock market crash poses particular challenges to the foundations that make grants to not-for-profit groups; the bear market has cut deeply into foundation endowments, prompting them to cut down the numbers of grants they make. But demand is rising for the services of charitable organizations in tough times—along with poverty levels and home foreclosure rates.

In the longer term, not-for-profits are expected to keep growing. For 2009 alone, not-for-profits were forecasting a need to fill 24,000 vacant or new jobs, according to the Bridgespan Group, a strategic consulting firm that works with not-for-profits,[2] with many of the openings in roles such as finance and fundraising. Not-for-profits responding to the Bridgespan survey reported that senior-level job openings were running 44 percent higher than shown in a poll taken in 2006. Perhaps more interesting, 21 percent of people hired between June 2007 and December 2008 were transitioning into the not-for-profit sector for the first time.

"All the data says there is a looming leadership deficit," says David Simms, managing partner of Bridgestar, an arm of Bridgespan that recruits managers for not-for-profit positions. "That's not to say there aren't talented people already in the not-for-profit sector, because there are. But in terms of supply and demand, you have older boomers leaving to retire or simply to do something new. So there will be a lot of positions to fill."

Simms advises job seekers not to target only not-for-profits where they have subject expertise or passion for the work involved. He says employers are looking for people with functional expertise in areas such as finance, technology, marketing and communications, and

A College Teacher Helps New Immigrants Adjust to America

Michelle McRae retired at age 64 from her first career teaching college-level English and French. She planned to stay in her home town of Fargo-Moorhead—the twin communities that straddle North Dakota and Minnesota—and spend time traveling with her husband and volunteering. But friends recruited her to volunteer with a new, very small not-for-profit group that provided language tutoring for new immigrants in the community. Before long, she found herself at the helm of the organization called Giving+Learning.

Fargo-Moorhead isn't known for its diversity. The community is 94 percent white and aging, with one out of every five residents over age 55. But over the past 10 years, the towns have seen an influx of about 3,700 refugees from more than 40 war-torn countries as part of a federal resettlement program that helps immigrants start new lives in the United States. The immigrants coming to Fargo-Moorhead arrive from countries such as Iraq, Somalia, Bosnia, and—most recently—Burundi. Most often they arrive with little knowledge of English or how to deal with everyday needs. At the outset, McRae had three volunteer language tutors who were 50 and older, but she quickly realized that the newcomers also needed help in other areas, such as filling out job applications, earning driver's licenses, and even shopping for groceries.

Giving+Learning has been a big hit in the community—the volunteer core has grown to 500, and it serves 600 immigrant arrivals at any given time. The program also has expanded to two additional nearby communities and works with more than 400 resource agencies to provide services to the newcomers. "It's such a simple concept, so doable and uncomplicated" McRae says. "You bring together the gifts and wisdom of our oldest generation with the needs of our newest citizens. It's a win-win situation."

McRae has expanded Giving+Learning into a volunteer operation of more than 500 people. The group has grown from its base in English-language tutoring to helping refugees get their high school equivalency diplomas, pass driver's license exams, and find jobs. Along the way, McRae has learned life-changing lessons about breaking down social barriers across age, culture, race, and ethnicity. "We are pretty much a white community and out of the mainstream, so the changes have caused some tensions," she notes. "But if you are helping someone and sitting across the kitchen table tutoring that person in English, it's difficult not to recognize that it's another human being. The connections have been very positive."

Now McRae is working on replicating Giving+Learning in other communities with new immigrant populations. She was recognized by Civic Ventures in 2008 as a recipient of its Purpose Prize, an annual cash award given to trailblazers who have demonstrated creative and effective work tackling social problems.

general management. But transitioning to not-for-profit work does require some recalibrated thinking. Job seekers should think about getting their feet wet by volunteering or serving on the board of a not-for-profit, which can be a great way to learn about cultural and organizational differences. Compensation also requires an adjustment. Pay probably will be somewhat lower than in the private sector, "but it's not like you have to survive on peanut butter," Simms says.

Expect to adjust your job-hunting strategy, too. Only 10 percent of not-for-profit openings are posted on any of the major online job boards, although Bridgestar operates a site for not-for-profit senior management jobs that it hopes will grow into a major portal for these opportunities. And most not-for-profit hiring is local; candidates generally aren't interested in relocating, and most employers don't have funds to pay for relocation. That makes local person-to-person networking the most important job-hunting tool, Simms says. "Friends serving on boards of [not-for-profits] can be a great networking tool. Also think about your alumni association or your university's career resources. [Not-for-profits] will often notify them of openings."

Resources

Bridgespan. This strategic consulting firm works with not-for-profits and maintains an online resource center (www.bridgespan.org/Careers/Default.aspx) on not-for-profit careers.

CommonGood Careers. This site (www.cgcareers.org/) offers help for both employers and job seekers in the world of social entrepreneurship.

Encore.org. Civic Ventures sponsors a social networking Web site (www.encore.org/) focused on midlife career transitions.

Experience Corps. Interested in tutoring? Experience Corps (www.experiencecorps.org/index.cfm) recruits adults over age 55 to mentor and tutor elementary students, with a focus on developing reading skills.

Idealist.org. This job board (http://idealist.org/) offers postings for a wide array of not-for-profit jobs and volunteer opportunities all over the world.

Partnership for Public Service. This not-for-profit organization (www.ourpublicservice.org/OPS/programs/fedexperience/index.shtml) works on an array of initiatives to recruit Americans to public service. In 2008, it launched an initiative focused on recruiting older workers called FedExperience Transitions to Government.

The Purpose Prize. Awarded annually by Civic Ventures, the Purpose Prize (www.purposeprize.org/index.cfm) provides five awards of $100,000 each to people 60 and older who are taking on society's biggest challenges. For inspiration, check out the detailed profiles and video interviews with prize winners.

Taproot Foundation. This not-for-profit group (www.taprootfoundation.org/) recruits marketing, human resources, and information-technology professionals for pro bono projects at not-for-profit groups—a great way to test the waters.

USAJobs. Find a comprehensive database of federal job openings at this official government site (www.usajobs.gov/).

Further Reading

Marc Freedman, *Encore: Finding Work That Matters in the Second Half of Life* (New York: PublicAffairs Books, 2007).

Chapter Notes

1. Bureau of Labor Statistics, "The Employment Situation, April 2009" (Washington, DC: U.S. Department of Labor, April 2009) (www.bls .gov/news.release/archives/empsit_05082009.pdf).
2. Bridgespan Group, *Finding Leaders for America's Nonprofits* (New York: The Bridgespan Group, 2009) (www.bridgespan .org/finding-leaders-for-americas-nonprofits.aspx), accessed May 20, 2009.

CHAPTER 17

Volunteering in Retirement
Getting Engaged

IN 2009, POLLSTER JOHN ZOGBY asked 4,000 Americans to answer this question: "What will be the historic legacy of baby boomers?" The responses were unflattering. Forty-two percent said boomers had "ushered in an era of consumerism and self-indulgence." Another 27 percent gave boomers credit for helping to "bring lasting change in social and cultural values and ending a war." After that, the answers ranged from "nothing really special" to "other" or "not sure."[1] The loose translation: "Your generation might have done some good things back in the 1960s and 1970s, but where have you been lately?"

The Greatest Generation. The Silent Generation. And now the Overindulgent, Self-Centered Generation. Doesn't sound too good, does it? It's an unfair and harsh assessment, to be sure. Still, many boomers are preparing to rewrite those poll results as they move into the next part of their lives. Even before the Great Recession began, many already were refocusing their energies on leaving a positive legacy for future generations. The trend has intensified as the country faces intense, simultaneous crisis and upheaval—a depressed economy, national security and environmental threats, and the need to revamp our health-care and education systems. "The needs in the country and in our communities are more stark and present and in the news," says John Gomperts, president of Civic Ventures, a not-for-profit think tank focused on civic engagement. "People are alert to the fact there are serious problems, and they are concerned." Indeed, one survey found that only 20 percent of boomers and members of the Silent Generation—those born during the Great Depression and World War II—believe they will leave the world in better condition than it was before, and 55 percent think they will leave the world in worse condition.[2]

In the last chapter, we looked at encore careers—transitions into second paid careers with social meaning. Now let's consider volunteer work—everything from helping out with a program at your church, synagogue, or mosque to going abroad with the Peace Corps.

Volunteering has been growing quickly in the United States and has hit a 30-year high point in recent years, with a good deal of the growth fueled by middle-aged and older adult volunteers.[3] The impulse toward public service and civic engagement is partly a response to the terrorist attacks on September 11, 2001, and natural disasters such as Hurricane Katrina and the 2004 tsunami.[4] But for some boomers who grew up in the political and social ferment of the 1960s and 1970s, civic engagement also is a natural return to first principles after decades spent developing careers, raising families, and funding big college-tuition bills (see—it wasn't all about self-indulgence!). One study found that 5.3 million to 8.4 million people between the ages of 44 and 70 are doing work that combines income and personal meaning with social impact; the study also noted that *half* of the people in this age group who are not already doing "work with meaning" see it as their future career direction.[5]

Civic engagement is getting a boost from Washington, too. President Barack Obama campaigned on a theme of civic engagement and national service in 2008, advocating expansion of existing programs such as the Peace Corps and the creation of new initiatives focused on education and energy. Obama and his Republican opponent, Senator John McCain, both lent their names to a new campaign promoting national service sponsored by a coalition of more than 100 not-for-profit organizations and corporations, including heavyweights such as the Carnegie Corporation, AARP, and Target. The Service Nation coalition's plan emphasizes service by older Americans, including a proposed Encore Service Corps that would provide opportunities in education, youth development, family and aging services, community and economic development, public health, and safety and environment.

Obama signed the Serve America Act in April 2009. The law sharply expands funding for community-service programs and creates new groups of volunteers focused on education, clean energy, health care, and veterans affairs. The law also includes funding to increase positions in programs such as AmeriCorps and funds programs for older Americans who want to work in not-for-profit organizations. It established a paid Encore Fellowships program for Americans age 55 or older in one-year management or leadership positions in not-for-profit organizations.

The not-for-profit sector's growth is another factor creating demand—and opportunity—for civic engagement and volunteer work. The total number of public charities in the United States grew 66 percent from 1995 to 2005, and their revenue and assets grew sharply as well.[6]

Then there's the recession. Out-of-work Americans have been volunteering at record levels as a way to keep busy and engaged while they hunt for paying jobs. Many of these volunteers are highly educated and skilled business professionals with a lot to offer not-for-profit groups, but many charities report that the new interest in volunteering is so strong that they've been forced to turn people away due to lack of capacity to manage and direct all the volunteer assistance.[7]

Altruism aside, volunteering offers a chance to learn new skills, feel valued, and leverage the skills learned in previous jobs. A study of Experience Corps tutors found that volunteers had better mental and physical health, more physical activity, and higher self-esteem as a result of their participation.[8] And if you're job hunting, volunteering can offer opportunities to network for your next position and try on new occupations for size. And if you go abroad, volunteering can literally open up the door to new cultures, experiences, and friendships beyond anything you've ever experienced.

Donna Miller: Learning to Appreciate Small Changes

When Donna Miller was about 50 years old, she started volunteering in an after-school program run by her church for ninth-grade students at Germantown High School in Philadelphia. She had heard a presentation about the program that mentioned that one-half of Germantown students dropped out of school before the end of ninth grade, and she felt compelled to join. "Having raised two girls myself, and having lots of nieces and nephews, I couldn't imagine what a ninth grader did who was not in school," she recalls.

Getting Started

So many social problems, so little time. So how should you go about finding your volunteer calling? Most people find themselves drawn to issues they've cared about for a long time. "I usually recommend that people try to listen to a calling," says Susan Skog, an expert who writes about volunteering. "If you really want a great long-term match, think about your passion—what has called to you for a long time, what have you always cared about, what wakes you up at night?"

Here's a checklist of questions to ponder before you leap, adapted from Susan's book, *The Give-Back Solution.*

1. Listen to your give-back call. What's it saying and asking of you? Tune into your inner compass and see where it leads you. Trust your instincts, your hunches for what feels right.
2. What brings you here now? Why is this the right time to act? Why now?
3. Are you drawn to a particular part of the country or of the world? Is there an area or region that's particularly compelling to you?
4. Do you want to make an impact right where you are? Is hands-on work in the trenches of Asia or Africa a turnoff for you? Do you feel more concerned about and drawn to helping out your local community or your country?
5. Do you want to get up close and personal? Are you sensing people and feeling the pull of connection? Is it necessary for you to work closely with the people you'll support?
6. Do you want an ongoing sense of community? Are you looking for a way to give back—and find camaraderie and a sense of community at the same time?
7. Do you want to find a group or organization with similar values and aims before you make a commitment?
8. Do you have a particular skill or sensibility you want to offer? Do you want to use your given profession to make a difference or feel you have a talent or gift that will lift up a part of the world?

9. Is there an issue that's captured your heart? Are you drawn to addressing a particular social, environmental, or economic challenge?

10. How flexible, nonjudgmental, and open-minded can you be? If you're choosing to go abroad, are you curious about other cultures?

11. Do you need external praise and rewards? Or can you be content with the internal satisfaction and knowledge that you made a difference?

12. Do you have the patience to go the distance? Whether volunteering overseas or engaging here, sometimes things don't move as fast as we'd like.

13. Do you have what it takes? Do you understand that even though humanitarian activism has become a hot pursuit, it should not be a half-hearted choice?

14. Are you ready to live at a deeper level? Are you ready for the adventure to begin?

Source: Susan Skog, *The Give-Back Solution*; © Sourcebooks, Inc., 2009; reprinted with permission.

Donna worked at the time as a marketing manager for a local software company and felt she could spare a bit of her free time. "I offered to come in and hand out snacks—that was all. But I came in the first day and was so struck by the energy of the kids—they really got to me. So I offered to run some arts programs. And I love to play games, so I found a bunch of logic games designed to really train your thinking and started bringing them in."

That was 10 years ago, and Donna hasn't looked back. "After that year, the kids didn't want to leave, so we devised a way to expand by starting an evening program that could draw more volunteers. We kept adding every year until we had kids coming all the way through their senior year." The program began with 40 children in its first year and has since expanded to serve 75 kids annually; 95 percent of the students graduate. Donna serves as the volunteer coordinator for the evening program.

The biggest lesson Donna has learned along the way about volunteer work is the importance of setting expectations properly. "Learn to appreciate the smallest amount of change you can see—don't look for the whole world to change just because you gave a day of your life to something. Celebrate the small changes, and be excited about what you can do." One of Donna's small wins was starting a cooking program—the kids all cook dinner together regularly as a social activity and learn healthy eating habits. Another win is a student who almost fell through the cracks after the death of his best friend from an asthma attack; today he works as a Philadelphia firefighter.

Volunteering has brought important changes to Donna's personal life. Several years ago, she reinvented her career after her employer went through several ownership changes that left Donna unsatisfied at work. She accepted a new position as administrator of the nation's first Methodist church, Historic St. George, in Philadelphia. The job pays far less than she made at the software company, but it leaves her the free time she needs for the youth program. "I just wanted to spend more time with those kids, and that made it much easier to make the decision to accept a lower-paying position."

Jeri Leedy: "Be Selfish about It"

Jeri Leedy has been volunteering most of her life. She taught Sunday school to 4-year-olds when she was just 10, and she volunteered at a hospital during high school. Later, when her husband was in the U.S. Army, she did a lot of volunteering with the American Red Cross. "We moved around so much, and it was always a great way to meet people. I wanted to be active in the community—and selfishly, I wanted to know the doctors who were seeing my children!"

Eventually, she settled in Jacksonville, Florida, where she mixed her paid work as an events manager with volunteer work for the Salvation Army. She retired from full-time work in 1999, and today at age 65 mixes volunteering with travel and time with family in Atlanta. She connected with the Salvation Army through the Senior Corps' RSVP volunteer network, which is operated by the Corporation for National and Community Service, the government-sponsored agency dedicated to fostering volunteerism.

"I would look for things that meshed with my background, and I tried a few things that didn't work. Then I signed up with the Salvation Army to help with Christmas programs—registering people for services, toys, and meals. I wound up being named volunteer of the year, which was embarrassing, because I didn't think I had done that much!"

She went on to get involved in the leadership of the local volunteer auxiliary and continues to devote substantial time as a volunteer. "If you have skills you can offer to an organization when you retire, it's a win-win," she says. "I enjoyed what I was doing and didn't really want to stop. If you can't do something related to your work, then be sure to find something that is going to challenge you a bit. You have to be kind of selfish about it."

Volunteering Abroad

If you'd like to travel the world and help make it a better place, a volunteer vacation could be right for you. Some people in the tourism industry call themselves *voluntourism* specialists—although that's a misnomer in the sense that volunteer travel will take you far beyond the experiences of typical tourism. Volunteering abroad is growing rapidly, and people are making a substantial commitment of time. One study found that 40 percent of all Americans would be interested in a volunteer-oriented trip lasting as long as three weeks; another 13 percent said they'd like to go abroad for as long as a year.[9] The trend has become large enough to support its own web portal, Voluntourism.org, a not-for-profit resource for educating travelers and connecting them with tour operators in the for-profit sector. Several for-profit travel websites also have jumped on the trend by offering voluntourism opportunities, including Travelocity and CheapTickets.com.

Voluntourism opportunities can last just a week or two, a couple of months, or much longer. Most programs charge a fee that covers the cost of your trip and helps the organization meet its overhead expenses; the fee is a charitable gift for tax purposes and hence is tax-deductible.

From a Bookstore to the Border of Tibet

Syrinda Sharpe was working at a university bookstore in Seattle when a friend sent an e-mail note suggesting that they go abroad together to do volunteer work. The friend forwarded a link to the Web site of Cross-Cultural Solutions (CCS), a not-for-profit organization that

Voluntourism: A Sampling of Organizations

You may not have two years to give to the Peace Corps, but there are still plenty of ways to give your time all over the world. Here's a small sampling of organizations.

Cross-Cultural Solutions. CCS (www.crossculturalsolutions.org/) places more than 4,000 volunteers annually in Africa, Asia, Latin America, and Eastern Europe. CCS prides itself on its ongoing in-country programs and infrastructure, and it boasts a worldwide staff of more than 300 people in 12 countries.

Globe Aware. This organization (www.globeaware.org/) places volunteers in more than 15 countries on a wide array of short-term volunteer projects focused on cultural awareness and sustainability.

Habitat for Humanity. Habitat's Global Village (www.habitat.org/gv/) sends team members to short-term house-building projects all over the world, with volunteers working alongside local residents.

World Teach Inc. Volunteers for World Teach (www.worldteach .org/) witness firsthand the challenges and rewards of education in a developing country, working as full-time teachers and as employees of their host school or sponsoring institution in their placement country. Most volunteers live with a host family or on the school campus and participate fully in the life of their host community. WorldTeach year programs are 10 to 12 months long.

sends volunteers to Africa, Asia, Latin America, and Eastern Europe. Syrinda, who was 50 at the time, had traveled extensively when she was younger but hadn't been outside the United States in 13 years. She was intrigued, and a serious discussion began about making a trip. Health problems ultimately prevented her friend from going, but Syrinda was hooked on the idea. "I didn't feel I was going anywhere in my career I'm in my fifties, and I thought: 'Do it now while you can.'"

She bought a book about volunteer travel and began investigating organizations that were listed online—but many were geared to "gap year" students and younger. CCS appealed for its broader age focus but also because "it didn't seem so protected from the cultural experience," she recalls. "I wanted the culture, education, and volunteering."

Like many of the top international volunteering organizations, CCS maintains operations in the locations where it sends volunteers, and new arrivals are plugged into ongoing work. CCS was started in the mid-1990s by Steve Rosenthal, a telecommunications engineer who had spent a year traveling in Nepal, India, Southeast Asia, Africa, and the Middle East. While in Kenya, he spent a week volunteering in a small village with a friend who was serving in the Peace Corps and was struck—hard—by experiencing the place as an involved inhabitant rather than as a tourist. His friend had been building a medical clinic in a small village, and Steve joined him for a week there, helping to build the clinic and making friends with many of the children for whom it was being made. That experience ultimately led him to start an organization in 1995 that could help others have that same experience. The initial focus was on volunteer work in India, expanding later to a much broader range of countries and regions.

Today, CCS is sending more than 4,000 volunteers abroad every year. Volunteers pay a fee that helps cover CCS overhead costs as well as the volunteer's travel expenses. Eight weeks of travel, for example, costs nearly $5,000. Volunteers are housed in a home-base location along with other workers—typically a house or group of apartments where everyone takes meals together. Volunteers also are encouraged to get out in the community on their own to experience the local culture.

Syrinda traveled to India in the fall of 2008, spending eight weeks in Dharamsala, a small city in northern India close to the border with Tibet; she was assigned to work with a women's group, where she taught English and basic computer skills. "That went fine, but it was festival season there, so many women were too busy to show up consistently."

Next Syrinda traveled to New Delhi, where she worked for another month in a 40-year-old program providing day care, education, and food for the families of impoverished migrant workers who come to the city to work on construction projects. She taught English and math to children ages 5 to 12 and oversaw their playtime. "I was really in my element there," she recalls. "I just fell in love—the kids were so amazing."

That second experience has stuck with her. "So often, I took for granted how much I had at home. You read about poverty and how people live elsewhere; but walking every day through the streets of New Delhi and standing in line with people at food carts to buy fruit, you find out that it's a different world out there. When I came home, the first time I went to my local grocery store, I couldn't move—I was standing there staring at this clean place, packed with food. I thought of all the people in India living in corrugated housing and the children who would get two meals a day, just grains or beans. And people are still happy. The women there had kids and worries, and some of the kids wore the same clothes all the time, but they always were happy and smiling and thrilled to see me. It just gives you a different perspective on how we look at happiness and others.

"Even a year later, it crosses my mind all the time that there are people I held in my arms who go hungry and don't have anything close to what I have."

The Peace Corps

Most people think of the Peace Corps as a young person's adventure, but 14 percent of volunteers are age 30 or older. There's no age limit on participation; the oldest volunteer turned 85 recently, and about 5 percent of volunteers are 50 or older.

The Peace Corps is the mother of all volunteering abroad programs, and it is going strong almost 50 years after President John F. Kennedy started it in 1961. Since then, more than 195,000 volunteers have worked in 139 countries all over the world. The program stands apart from any other volunteer program because of the depth of commitment it requires, its prestige, and the fact that the program actually pays you—a little.

The Peace Corps application process is competitive; in 2008, there were 13,000 applicants, and only one in three was accepted. A network of full-time recruiters around the United States interviews every applicant; if accepted, you'll need to pass a rigorous medical exam—and it's the same exam no matter your age. However, if you do have medical conditions or special risks, the Peace Corps will take that into account by placing you in a location with access to good medical facilities or where you can avoid any special environmental risks for you, such as food allergies or weather.

Peace Corps volunteers live and work abroad for twenty-seven months, including three months of in-country training that includes learning about safety and security, language and cultural issues, and work-related skills. Some volunteers have their own quarters, and others live with local host families; married couples can be placed together. You'll receive a small living allowance, full medical and dental care, and travel expenses to and from your assignment.

Shirley and Danny Sherrod applied in 2006. Danny had retired in 1999 after selling a small manufacturing business in Fort Worth, Texas. Shirley retired in 2000 from her job as a nurse practitioner. They were young—he was 47, and she 50—and traveled around the United States for several years in a recreational vehicle, working some of the time as volunteers for the U.S. Bureau of Land Management and in the national parks.

When they applied to join the Peace Corps, Shirley was 55 and Danny 53. "We had traveled a great deal throughout the developing world and always enjoyed meeting people," says Danny. "We also had met a number of Peace Corps volunteers, and it seemed to us that as a traveler, you only get to meet local people at the most basic level. We wanted to really make friends and get to know people and the local culture."

The Sherrods initially were posted to the Republic of Suriname in South America but were reassigned after six months to western Panama when Suriname's extreme heat led to some health problems for Shirley. In Panama, both teach English as a second language; Danny also helps train others to teach English at a local university, and he helps with programs promoting local tourism. Shirley works with a local women's group that provides job training for low-income women, and she's developing a birth-control program.

Older volunteers sometimes encounter difficulties with family members who don't understand their decision to ship off to parts unknown, but that wasn't an issue for the Sherrods, who have three adult children from earlier marriages ranging in age from 30 to 41. "Our children were used to us taking off and doing things and being out of touch a couple months at a time," says Shirley. But she does admit that it can be difficult being separated from her grandchildren, ages 11, 13, and 17.

Other challenges associated with age? One is language. The Sherrods spent six weeks in Guatemala in an intensive Spanish program, and they continued their studies in Panama. "We get by pretty well, but it is harder to learn a new language as you get older," Shirley says.

But benefits have far outweighed the challenges. Says Danny, "The Peace Corp slogan used to be 'The toughest job you will ever love.' Even though they don't use the slogan any more, it's an incredibly accurate description of the work that volunteers do. Peace Corps is a great experience that tests you on a seemingly endless number of levels."

Adds Shirley, "The benefits are very personal for each individual. You get the satisfaction of helping someone less fortunate or maybe just attaining your own goals. You learn about a new culture and language, and you are active and productive. You truly do make friends with people of another culture in a way that would never happen as tourists or even as ex-pats."

The Sherrods' Peace Corps stint ends in August 2011. What next? "We might try to stay in the Peace Corps by becoming a country director, trainer, or recruiter," Danny says. "Or maybe we'll go back to our old life in the RV."

Resources

Volunteering in the United States

AARP. The AARP maintains an online volunteering resource center (www.aarp.org/makeadifference/volunteer/).

All for Good. This volunteer-opportunity postings Web site (http://www.allforgood.org/) was created by Silicon Valley techies.

Experience Corps. This program (www.experiencecorps.org/index.cfm) provides tutoring and mentoring opportunities for elementary school students who are struggling with learning to read. Now operating in 23 cities, the program is supported by public and private funders.

Experience Wave. This project (www.experiencewave.org/) works to advance federal and state policies that ease the transition of midlife and older adults to community-oriented work.

Get Involved. This Corporation for National & Community Service Web site (www.getinvolved.gov/) focuses on baby boomer volunteering.

SCORE. A nonprofit association, SCORE matches older volunteer business professionals with mentoring opportunities (www.score.org/).

Senior Corps. This organization (www.seniorcorps.gov/) connects older Americans with opportunities to mentor, coach, or contribute their job skills and expertise to community projects and organizations.

Serve.gov. This volunteering resource site (www.serve.gov/) is maintained by the Corporation for National and Community Service.

The New Service. This is a blog (http://thenewservice.wordpress .com/) that seeks to catalyze citizen service. It is a joint project of staff members from Idealist.org, Northwest Regional Educational Laboratory, the Corporation for National and Community Service, the National Service Inclusion Project, and Innovations in Civic Participation.

Volunteering Abroad

Cross Cultural Solutions. This international organization (www .crossculturalsolutions.org/), which has no political or religious affiliations, operates volunteer programs around the world in partnership with sustainable community initiatives.

Peace Corps 50+. This resource Web site (www.peacecorps.gov/ minisite/50plus/index.cfm) is maintained by the Peace Corps for older volunteers and includes video interviews with 50-plus volunteers and frequently asked questions.

Travel for Good. This Travelocity Web site (http://www.travelocity .com/TravelForGood/index.html) showcases a program that offers grants to subsidize volunteer vacations.

Voluntourism.org. This not-for-profit resource (www.voluntourism .org/) educates travelers and connects them with tour operators in the for-profit sector.

Further Reading

Dillon Banergee, *The Insider's Guide to the Peace Corps: What to Know Before You Go* (Berkeley, CA: Ten Speed Press, 2009).

David Bornstein, *How to Change the World: Social Entrepreneurs and the Power of New Ideas* (New York: Oxford University Press, 2007).

Bill McMillon, Doug Cutchins, and Anne Geissinger, *Volunteer Vacations: Short-Term Adventures That Will Benefit You and Others* (Chicago: Chicago Review Press, 2009).

Susan Skog, *The Give-Back Solution: Create a Better World with Your Time, Talents and Travel (Whether You Have $10 or $10,000)* (Chicago: Sourcebooks, 2009).

Chapter Notes

1. John Zogby, "The Baby Boomers' Legacy," Forbes.com (July 23, 2009) (www.forbes.com/2009/07/22/baby-boomer-legacy-change -consumer-opinions-columnists-john-zogby.html), accessed August 2009.

2. John M. Bridgeland, Robert D. Putnam, and Harris L. Wofford, *More to Give: Tapping the Talents of the Baby Boomer, Silent and Greatest Generations* (Washington, DC: AARP, 2008), p. 14 (www .civicenterprises.net/pdfs/aarp_moretogive.pdf), accessed August 2009.

3. Robert Grimm Jr., Nathan Dietz, John Foster-Bey, David Reingold, and Rebecca Nesbit, *Volunteer Growth in America: A Review of Trends Since 1974* (Washington, DC: Corporation for National and Community Service, December 2006), p. 2 (www.nationalservice.gov/ about/role_impact/performance_research.asp#VOLGROWTH), accessed August 2009.

4. Grimm et al., p. 5.

5. MetLife/Civic Ventures, *Encore Career Survey* (Washington, DC/ San Francisco: MetLife/Civic Ventures, 2008) (www.civicventures.org/ publications/surveys/encore-career-survey.cfm), accessed August 2009.

6. Amy Blackwood, Kennard T. Wing, and Thomas H. Pollak, *The Nonprofit Sector in Brief: Facts and Figures from the Nonprofit Almanac 2008* (Washington, DC: Urban Institute Press, National Center for Charitable Statistics, 2008) (http://nccs.urban.org/statistics/quickfacts.cfm), accessed August 2009

7. Meredith May, "Charities Tap Skills of Jobless Professionals," *San Francisco Chronicle* (March 23, 2009) (www.sfgate.com/cgi-bin/article.cgi?file=/c/a/2009/03/23/MNPB16JHP3.DTL), accessed August 2009.

8. Nancy Morrow-Howell, Song-Iee Hong, Stacey McCrary, and Wayne Blinne, *Experience Corps: Health Outcomes of Participation* (St. Louis: Washington University, George Warren Brown School of Social Work, February 2009) (www.experiencecorps.org/impact/for_members.cfm), accessed August 2009.

9. Henry DeVries, "Popularity Grows for 'Voluntourism,'" press release, University of California–San Diego (April 9, 2008) (http://ucsdnews.ucsd.edu/newsrel/general/04-08Voluntourism.asp), accessed August 2009.

CHAPTER 18

Learning and the Path to Brain Fitness

NANCY MERZ NORDSTROM NEVER planned to be an educator. But the self-described traditional wife and mother woke up one morning in 1993—at age 48—to find that her husband had died in his sleep of a heart attack. After some time passed, she decided to go back to school to help get her life on track. "I wanted to sit down with women like myself and share our experiences. But the only grief programs I could find were in cold, clinical settings like hospitals. I wanted a nice living room setting where younger widows like myself could get together and talk about how to remake our lives. Since I couldn't find one, I decided to start one myself—and then realized I needed to go back to school because I didn't know anything about running a grief counseling group."

With four children to raise, she put education on the back burner for a few years. But at age 51, Nancy did go back to school, intending to become a grief counselor. But she found her focus shifting to the learning process itself. "I found that the sheer act of learning was just an incredible experience. I was at a nontraditional college where the students all were working adults, and we took classes in the evening. We had people with varying amounts of education who wanted to move up in the business world. Seeing what it did for them—and for me—showed me the value of continuing to learn and what a difference education could make in my life."

Nancy's plans changed. She wound up getting a master's in adult education, eventually going to work for Elderhostel, one of the nation's premier adult learning organizations. Today she directs the Elderhostel Institute Network, the largest educational network for older adults in

North America. She's also one of the nation's top experts and advocates for lifelong learning.

Heading back to the classroom has long been popular as an enrichment activity in retirement. But, as Nancy learned, adult learning can transform lives and lead to new careers. It's also becoming clear that keeping the brain challenged is beneficial to health and general well-being.

The concept of brain fitness has caught fire in recent years, with much of the attention focused on software programs and games that claim to help older people maintain mental acuity and blunt the cognitive decline associated with aging. Nancy is a skeptic. "You can use mind software on your own—I don't have any problem with it," she says. "It's just that you also need to get out of the house and stay active. It's as simple as 'use it or lose it.' If we want to do everything possible to keep our whole being alert, vibrant, and connected as we age, we have to continue to challenge ourselves."

Learning activities stimulate the brain, producing benefits such as enhanced mental alertness, thought processes, response times, and reflexes.[1] "When you look at the benefits gained from keeping your mind sharp, it's incredible," Merz Nordstrom says. "Lifelong learning is like a health club for your brain."

Another important benefit is participation in a community of like-minded learners. "People come for the learning, but they stay for the community that they find," says Judy Mann, director of the Osher Lifelong Learning Institute (LLI) at Northwestern University's School of Continuing Studies. "This gets more important as people unplug from connections professionally, because they can find like-minded people in learning communities."

Americans appear to be getting the message; adult learning programs are proliferating quickly, feeding everything from hobbies to career retraining. "What we find is that people want to study the things they never had time for before," Merz Nordstrom says. "If their college years were focused on a career, now they want to study liberal arts or an artistic endeavor. The humanities are very big, especially history."

And not all that learning is going on in classrooms. Educational travel and learning-oriented community service programs also play key roles. "For most people, it will just be a question of how involved, how focused?" Mann says. "How big a part of your life do you want to make this?"

The Landscape

Adult learners can choose from a very broad array of programs, including Lifelong Learning Institutes, continuing education, and educational travel.

Lifelong Learning Institutes. These are self-directed learning communities organized and run by members, most of whom are 50 or older. LLIs usually are operated under the auspices of a college or university, and their numbers have grown rapidly in recent years, partly because of the work of the Bernard Osher Foundation, a California-based philanthropy that supports educational and arts programs. Osher has funded a network of Osher Lifelong Learning Institutes at 120 colleges and universities around the country. The LLI movement is very bottom-up and member directed, and community is just as important as curriculum.

Continuing education. Career retrainers are flocking to community colleges and other postsecondary campuses for job training and career transformation. Community colleges trace their roots to training teachers and nurses in the early 1900s; they later accommodated World War II veterans studying on the GI Bill and then expanded to offer a broader vocational curriculum as baby boomers went to college in the 1960s.[2] Now community colleges are gearing up to help midlife adults retrain for an array of second careers. They're focusing on fields such as teaching, health care, social services, and entrepreneurial start-ups. Civic Ventures has awarded grants to community colleges around the country to spur experimentation with new programs targeting midlife learners, and the American Association of Community Colleges is funding demonstration projects as part of a three-year Plus 50 Initiative.[3]

Educational travel. Elderhostel is the great-grandparent on the block. Started in the late 1960s, it was the country's first not-for-profit educational travel organization and remains the largest, with more than 8,000 programs in 90 countries. Elderhostel adopted a new name for its travel programs in 2009—Exploritas—to address a problem the organization had marketing to baby boomers; the programs were a great fit with boomer interests, but that "E" word? Not so much. Exploritas's success has inspired other well-regarded educational travel organizations, some of which offer more specialized programs.[4] For example, Elder-Treks takes 50-plus clients on adventure travel trips in more than 80 countries. Immersion programs abroad can help you gain fluency in the language of your choice. The Smithsonian Institution operates a large museum-based educational travel program, Smithsonian Journeys.

Blending education and travel can deepen your engagement with the places you visit. Like other forms of adult learning, it also provides a sense of shared community between you and other like-minded learners.

Going Abroad to Study a Language

Immersion language-study programs have proliferated quickly over the past few years, offering plenty of opportunities to improve fluency—quickly—in the language of your choice.

Amerispan Study Abroad. With roots in Spanish-language study, this 15-year-old program has since expanded to offer 15 languages in more than 45 countries throughout the Americas, Europe, Asia, the Middle East, Australia, and Africa. It also offers specialized programs for professionals in specific disciplines, volunteering, and internship programs (http://amerispan.com).

Bridge-Linguatec. This organization (www.bridgeabroad.com/adults.php) offers immersion language, volunteering, and service learning programs and opportunities to teach English abroad. Immersion language programs are focused on Central and South America and Europe.

Learning Destinations. This company (http://learningdestinations.com/) offers language immersion, fine arts, cooking, and volunteer opportunities.

Learning Vacations

Summer institutes and camps can be a great way to vacation and learn at the same time; think of them as summer camps for grown-ups.

Aspen Ideas Festival. The prestigious Aspen Institute runs an annual summer festival (www.aifestival.org/) that draws heavy hitters from the arts, government, science, and business. Aspen says it wants to draw people interested in "stepping out of their day-to-day routines to challenge themselves and learn about their world and the ideas that are shaping it."

Chautauqua Institution. The Chautauqua Institution is one of the nation's oldest institutions dedicated to adult learning. Its "55+ Residential Weeks" runs in conjunction with Exploritas (www.ciweb .org/55exploritas/).

ElderTreks. This organization (www.eldertreks.com/index.php) offers adventure travel tailored for the 50-plus tourism market.

Exploritas. Formerly known as Elderhostel, Exploritas (www .exploritas.org/) is the great-grandparent of educational travel programs with more than 8,000 programs in 90 countries.

Smithsonian Journeys. This is the world's largest museum-based educational travel program (www.smithsonianjourneys.org/).

A Politician Learns Some New Tricks

Dick Phelan spent much of his career in the rough and tumble of Chicago's legal and political worlds. He's an attorney with more than 40 years of experience in the courtroom and running his own law firms. In 1990, he was elected to a term as president of the Cook County Board of Commissioners, which oversees a vast system of courts, jails, and public-health delivery in the Chicago metropolitan area. In 1988–1989, he took a turn in the national spotlight as special outside counsel to the congressional investigation of House Speaker James C. Wright Jr., who subsequently resigned from office.

Shortly after retiring a few years ago at age 69, Phelan decided to check out the Osher LLI at Northwestern University, but he was skeptical about the student-directed format: "A class where students did all the talking? Would that mean the person who yaps the most dominates the class? Would you really learn anything?"

But he was pleasantly surprised by the quality of discussion. "I wound up in a class on foreign affairs with someone who had been a foreign service officer—he's lived in Moscow, London, and Paris and was in Vietnam during the war there. There was another person who was familiar with Pakistan; he'd served in the Peace Corps there and later worked there as a contractor. So we had these people sprinkled through the class who would just raise their hands and talk about their experience. You couldn't go to Harvard or Yale and find people that smart with those kinds of experiences. So I got pretty excited."

These days, he spends two days a week—four hours daily—in classes covering subjects such as foreign affairs, economics, history, and politics. "That's a lot of hours, but everyone is here for one purpose, to learn. I really like the approach—there's a coordinator who picks the books; but the students run the class, pick out the questions for discussion and the articles we read. It's very interactive."

Phelan is a graduate of Georgetown University Law School and the University of Notre Dame and says, "I work as hard preparing for these classes as I ever did in law school. It's just become a life unto itself. You've got to exercise your mind to keep it going—the last thing any of us want to do is fall into senility!"

Creativity, Learning, and Positive Aging

Jeanne Kelly is a professional singer, conductor, and pianist who has worked for many years with major opera companies and symphonies in the Washington-Baltimore area, where she lives. In 2001, she was directing the Levine School of Music's Arlington, Virginia, program when Dr. Gene Cohen approached her with an idea.

Dr. Cohen, who died in 2009, was one of the nation's leading researchers on the effects that creativity can have on older adults and the aging process. He directed the Center on Aging, Health, and Humanities at George Washington University, where he was a professor of health-care sciences, psychiatry, and behavioral sciences. Cohen helped to create a national movement around positive aging and argued against the old stereotype that aging leads inevitably to a decline in physical and mental capacity. His pioneering research demonstrated that life after 65 can be an important period of creativity and intellectual growth.

Cohen wanted to talk with Kelly about a new research project that would attempt to measure the impact on older adults of participation in a professionally run arts organization. He asked Kelly to help get the project started by forming several chorales for older adult singers that he could study. She'd need to start two new singing groups to join with a seniors' chorale she already was directing at a local senior living facility.

Kelly formed the groups, which embarked on an ambitious and professionally oriented program of rehearsal and performance. Cohen's research—conducted over a three-year period—focused on comparing the singing seniors with control groups that didn't participate in similar activities. The key finding: Sustained involvement in Kelly's program resulted in a measurable, positive impact on overall health and longevity, doctor visits, medication use, falls, loneliness, and morale.[5]

Meanwhile, Kelly—who was 51 herself when she first got involved in Cohen's work—got hooked on arts programs for older adults. In 2007, she founded a not-for-profit organization called Encore Creativity for Older Adults to manage and develop the senior chorales. "I decided that I wanted to simply do art for older adults. We've expanded enormously since then, which tells me that people are retiring and they want sophistication, and that they want to carry on what they were doing in their careers or find something wonderful they have never done before."

When Kelly first formed the chorales, the average singer's age was 80, and many of them are still singing with Kelly 10 years later. Chorales have been formed in 10 locations around the Washington-Baltimore area, with singers ranging in age from 55 to 97. Encore Chorales are "no-cut"—anyone can join—but they're dead serious about performance and professionalism. "Some have a background in singing, and some have never sung in their lives—someone at some point told them, 'You shouldn't sing.' But if you teach someone to sing they will get it. We just seat them next to someone who is strong." The chorales rehearse for two 15-week sessions each year; they give eight concerts in May and another eight each December. Their performing venues include the John F. Kennedy Center for the Performing Arts and the Smithsonian American Art Museum. Encore Creativity for Older Adults also runs camps for singers at the Chautauqua Institution in upstate New York and at St. Mary's College of Maryland and a dance-and-movement program in Arlington, Virginia. Most recently, Kelly launched a singing program designed for residents of assisted-living facilities. "I hated the idea of assisted living being a real dead end, especially artistically," she says. "Many people are there because of mobility problems, and the program has had excellent results."

Writing the Great American Novel

Rita Dragonette had a long, successful career in public relations and ran an independent agency in Chicago with her late husband, Joe. She sold the business to a larger global agency in 1999 toward the end of Joe's long struggle with multiple sclerosis and left the industry about two years later.

At age 50, she was headed back to school. "I majored in English in college and always thought of myself as a writer. But that was always on the back burner during my career because the public relations business was so consuming. I knew I would write when I retired from the business, but I also knew that I couldn't go to an unstructured environment. After working in a business with deadline writing for 30 years, you need accountability!"

Rita decided to enroll at the Writers Studio at the University of Chicago Graham School of General Studies. She started off with a couple of classes in literature and writing and then applied for admission to a program leading to a writing certificate. She spent two years completing the certificate and has been participating in writers' workshops all over the world since then.

She's been working on a novel about the political tumult surrounding the Vietnam War. "It's set in 1969 and 1970—the time frame of the first draft lottery and the shootings at Kent State. My protagonist is a young woman whose birthday would have come up number one in the draft, if women had been included in the lottery system." When we spoke in the summer of 2009, she was finishing it up with the help of a writing coach. Her next step: shopping for a publisher.

The cultural transition from business to the classroom was difficult. "I had run a company, and classes just aren't run in an orderly, business-like way. You have to sit through a lot of inefficiency, like when a professor lets a student grandstand or make inappropriate comments. Sometimes I wanted to just jump up and grab the teacher and say 'Do it like this!'"

Starting over after all that time at the top of a profession posed another challenge. "You might have a great idea for a novel but don't have the craft to realize it because you haven't been working at this for 25 years. It's a huge ego transition to hear a teacher say that what you've written has a long way to go. You have to share your writing, and it's like being naked on a football field full of spectators—you're very vulnerable."

But Rita did find a supportive community of other writers and that's been the biggest reward in returning to school as an adult. "You start off in a class of ten or fifteen, but then you find two or three people you can really relate to and share your work. That helps because the loneliest thing is trying to do this on your own. When you interact with people it's just great—it gives you a community. It also opened the door to all the conferences and workshops I've been attending since then, and I've met incredible people there as well."

Resources

Encore Creativity. Encore Creativity for Older Adults (http://encorecreativity.org) is Jeanne Kelly's program for senior singers in the Washington, DC, area.

Lifelong Learning Institutes. These are self-directed learning programs via Exploritas, formerly Elderhostel (www.exploritas.org/ein/learning_na.asp).

International LLI programs. This directory to Lifelong Learning Institutes available outside the United States (www.usm.maine.edu/olli/national/links/international.jsp) is maintained by the Osher Lifelong Learning Institute's National Resource Center.

OASIS Institutes. These not-for-profit learning and volunteer service institutes are part of a network that offers programs in 25 cities (www.oasisnet.org/).

Bernard Osher Foundation. This charitable foundation (www .osherfoundation.org/) funds institutions of lifelong learning.

Learning Later, Living Greater. Nancy Merz Nordstrom publishes this useful Web site (www.learninglater.com/) about lifelong learning.

SeniorNet Technology. This Web site (www.seniornet.org/jsnet/index .php?option=com_frontpage&Itemid=1) helps older adults explore educational opportunities.

Shepherd's Centers of America. This network of interfaith community-based organizations (www.shepherdcenters.org/) provides meaning and purpose for adults throughout their mature years.

Travel Program Directory. This list of programs with an educational focus is maintained at Osher LLI's National Resource Center (www.usm .maine.edu/olli/national/links/travel_resources_educational_focus.jsp).

Further Reading

Gene D. Cohen, *The Mature Mind: The Positive Power of the Aging Brain* (New York: Basic Books, 2006).
Nancy Merz Nordstrom and Jon F. Merz, *Learning Later, Living Greater: The Secret for Making the Most of Your After-50 Years* (Boulder, CO: Sentient Publications, 2006).

Chapter Notes

1. Nancy Merz Nordstrom and Jon F. Merz, *Learning Later, Living Greater: The Secret for Making the Most of Your After-50 Years* (Boulder, CO: Sentient Publications, 2006), p. 25.
2. David Bank, "Encore Colleges" (Washington, DC/San Francisco: Civic Ventures/MetLife Foundation, 2007) (www.civicventures .org/communitycolleges/Encore_Colleges.pdf), accessed September 2009.
3. Kelly Greene, "Savvy Schools," *Wall Street Journal* (April 17, 2009) (http://online.wsj.com/article/SB123972559135117421.html#pr), accessed September 2009.

4. Merz Nordstrom and Merz, p. 159.

5. Gene D. Cohen, Susan Perlstein, Jeff Chapline, Jeanne Kelly, Kimberly M. Firth, and Samuel Simmens, "The Impact of Professionally Conducted Cultural Programs on the Physical Health, Mental Health, and Social Functioning of Older Adults," *The Gerontologist* (December 2006) (www.ncbi.nlm.nih.gov/pubmed/17169928?dopt=Abstract), accessed August 2009.

About the Author

Mark Miller is an award-winning journalist and consultant who specializes in retirement and aging. He writes the weekly syndicated newspaper column "Retire Smart" and is a contributor to The Huffington Post and CBS MoneyWatch.com. He also edits and publishes Retirement Revised.com, which offers advice on retirement planning, investing, and careers.

The former editor of *Crain's Chicago Business* and Sunday editor of the *Chicago Sun-Times*, Miller has reported extensively on money and career issues, and he has been a regular business news commentator on television and radio.

Mark Miller lives near Chicago with his wife, Anita. They have three grown children: Shira, Beth, and Asher.

Index

AARP, 88
  Best Employers for Workers Over
    50, 126, 143
  job resources, 143
  reverse mortgage calculator, 102
  volunteer resource center, 194
  working pros and cons, 123
Accenture, 136
Accumulation phase, 44
Adult learning. *See* Brain fitness;
    Education; Lifelong learning
Age disclosure, on résumé, 142
Age discrimination, 8, 130–131
Age Discrimination in Employment
    Act of 1967, 130
Aging in Community directory, 103
Aging in place, 94–98
All for Good, 194
Alzheimer's patients, 97
American Association of Community
    Colleges, 201
American Association of Homes and
    Services for the Aging, 99
American Institute of Certified
    Public Accountants, 111
Amerispan Study Abroad, 202
Angel investors, 150
Annuities
  deferred, 44
  fixed life, 20
  flexibility and simplicity of, 43
  income, 5, 41–48
Arthur Andersen, 136
Arts programs, 204–206
Aspen Ideas Festival, 203
Asset allocation
  glide path, 55
  imbalances in, 54
Asset management, 401(k)
    performance and, 52

Automated phone systems, 96
Automatic IRA, 32, 56–57
Automobile driving, 97

Baby boomers
  legacy of, 9–10, 183–184
  as market, 147
Beacon Hill Village Model, 97–98,
    100, 102–103
Bernard Osher Foundation,
    201, 208
Best Employers for Workers Over 50
    (AARP), 126–127, 143
Bizstarters, 146, 153, 164
Bloomberg BusinessWeek, 156
Boeing, 125
Bolles, Richard N., 161
Bolles workshops, 161
Boot camps, 160
Brain drain, 125–126
Brain fitness, 199–208
  creativity, learning, and positive
    aging, 204–206
  examples, 203–204, 206–207
  language study abroad, 202–203
  programs, 201–203
  resources, 207–208
Break-even age, 24
Bridge-Linguatec, 202
Bridgespan Group, 178, 181
Bridgestar, 178, 180
Bright Green Talent, 177
Brookings Institution, 56
Brown, Al, 152–155
Burnout, 134
Business formation, 9, 146. *See also*
    50+ entrepreneurs

Campbell, Anita, 150
CareerBuilder, 143

213